FACING
FINANCIAL
FEARS

8 STEPS TO FINANCIAL FREEDOM FOR WOMEN

by

Sarah L. Carlson CLU, CHFC, CFP®

Facing Financial Fears

Sarah Carlson
Spokane, WA
Lovemoneyjournal@gmail.com

Ordering Information:
Special discounts are available on quantity purchases by corporations, associations, educational institutions, and others. For details, contact Sarah Carlson above.
Printed in the United States of America
First Edition
Hardcover ISBN 978-1-5136-9517-4
Softcover ISBN 978-1-5136-9516-7
eBook ISBN 978-1-5136-9515-0
Library of Congress

Publisher
Winsome Entertainment Group LLC
Sandy, UT

In Gratitude

I dedicate this book to my sister, Brenda, who has been with me every step of the way and gives me valuable input.

To my husband, Andy, you have allowed me to be myself and to go after my dreams and goals. Thank you for the life we share.

To my children, William, Ben, Charlie, and Sue, you give me lift to be my best. I am so proud of each of you.

Thank you to my family, friends, and colleagues who have encouraged me on my journey.

"Life is an opportunity, benefit from it.

Life is a beauty, admire it.

Life is bliss, taste it.

Life is a dream, realize it.

Life is a challenge, meet it.

Life is a duty, complete it.

Life is a game, play it.

Life is costly, care for it.

Life is wealth, keep it.

Life is love, enjoy it.

Life is mystery, know it.

Life is a promise, fulfill it.

Life is a sorrow, overcome it.

Life is a song, sing it.

Life is a struggle, accept it.

Life is a tragedy, confront it.

Life is an adventure, dare it.

Life is luck, make it.

Life is too precious, do not destroy it.

Life is Life, fight for it!."

- Mother Teresa

TABLE OF CONTENTS

WHAT ARE YOU *REALLY* AFRAID OF?

Divorce is never easy, but Claudia had one consolation at least: she got the house.

And what a beautiful house it was: four bedrooms, three bathrooms, a family room, a library, a gourmet kitchen, a big backyard – just the right size for Claudia, her two kids, and anyone who might visit. Situated in one of the city's most prestigious neighborhoods, this house – *her* house – made her feel good about herself. *Look at all I've achieved,* it seemed to say. *I may be single, but I'm a woman of means.*

When she came to my office, though, Claudia was a hot mess, terrified of losing all that she had won. Without her ex-husband's income, she struggled to make her payments and to afford the maintenance costs – a new water heater, a badly needed paint job. To keep up, she'd taken on a second job, which meant missing her kids' football and basketball games as well as social time with her friends, so important for support after her divorce.

"I feel like a hamster on a wheel," she said to me. "I'm working twenty-four/seven just to make ends meet, and it's not enough." She had little money for anything extra. Groceries, clothes, and school supplies for her children took up the rest, leaving her almost nothing for herself. "I can't take a third job," she said. "I'd never see my kids at all."

After looking at the numbers, I made a suggestion: why not sell the house and downsize?

"Absolutely not," she said, almost before I'd finished my sentence. She wanted to give her kids some continuity – after all, their home had just been broken. Theirs was a nice neighborhood, conveniently close to her primary workplace and their school.

And besides, she said, she *loved* her house. She'd fought hard for it in the divorce. Why would she give it up?

Claudia's excuses might have sounded good to someone who didn't know better. But I've been a financial planner for too long not to see through her stories. Claudia had rejected my idea not because she loved her house so much – another house could be just as lovable – but out of fear.

She feared another big change, not just for her kids but for herself as well, on the heels of such a tumultuous time.

She feared losing face with her community of friends, who openly admired what they jokingly called her "mansion."

She feared seeming wishy-washy or even unstable to her ex as well as to her kids, by letting go after fighting for, and winning, the house.

And most of all, she feared the loss of her identity to herself, an identity tied up in being the woman who "had it all," meaning her "dream house."

But as I explained to her, Claudia's house had become more a source of stress than pleasure for her. Money worries kept her up at night. She needed a vacation, but having to pour so much income into her house, she couldn't afford to take one even with her children. And, as much as she loved the house, how much time was she able to spend there, and how much energy did she have to enjoy it?

I wondered which her children might prefer: staying in their big house without their mother around, or moving to another, smaller place where she could be home at night? Claudia felt confident that they would want to stay. But that's not what happened.

Her kids said they wanted more of their mom. Plus, they'd noticed her exhaustion from working all the time. The house, they said, meant little to them.

"You could have knocked me over with a feather," Claudia said – but *I* was not surprised.

With my guidance, Claudia put together a post-divorce plan. In a few months, she had sold her house and bought another, smaller home in the same school district. This change enabled her to cut her weekly work hours to forty, with evenings and weekends free to spend at home, visiting with friends and attending her kids' sports games and other events.

The budget she set enabled her to have more discretionary income than when she had worked two jobs, and she took the kids that year on their first family trip since the divorce.

When I saw her after these changes, she looked better than I had ever seen her: radiant and relaxed, her good sleep having returned at night.

The Many Faces of Fear

Claudia's story is not unusual. I see it all the time: people, especially women, paralyzed by fear and stuck in a bad situation. Often, they think they don't have enough money to live their dreams, so they work harder and harder, burning themselves out without achieving anything. Or they may already have all the money they need but cannot enjoy it, fearful of losing it all.

People manifest their money fears in so many ways, none of them healthy.

One person spends recklessly, racking up debt, and then over-drawing their accounts because they are afraid to look at their balances.

Another dreams of traveling and has ample money invested, but cannot bring themselves to book a trip – because what if something happens, and they need the money?

Someone else grew up in poverty and, although successful now, is always struggling to pay bills because their fear of feeling deprived keeps them from setting a budget.

Fear Is Just a Story We Tell Ourselves

The common denominator for these people and many others like them: their money stories are keeping them from living their best lives.

We all have money stories. They're a part of the vast compilation of tales that we tell ourselves about ourselves every day, stories such as, "I'm terrible at math," (forgetting about the terrible teacher we had in the fourth grade), "I'm not a morning person," (because we're up late every night binge-watching), and so on.

Our stories can help us survive in tough times. Telling ourselves that we actually enjoy being alone can be helpful during a lockdown.

Too often, though, our self-stories limit us. If we succumb to our fear of flying, we'll have a hard time taking that bucket list trip to Machu Picchu. Why not meditate and learn to calm our anxieties and call ourselves "adventuresome" instead?

So many of us have bound our identities with things we own or lifestyles we lead: the fashion plate, the jetsetter, the adventure hound, the corporate executive, even the starving artist. But neither our possessions nor our lifestyle makes us who we are. The stories we tell ourselves can be more fantasy than fact.

What stories do you tell yourself about money? Chances are, they took root in your psyche when you were young. You may not even be aware of them – yet.

Fear of Depriving Ourselves

Molly grew up with parents who'd both lived in poverty as children. Because each parent dealt with their past differently, each gave her conflicting messages about money.

Her father pinched every penny, hoarding his money out of a fear of becoming destitute. Asking him for anything had filled Molly with dread.

Her mother had grown up wearing clothes that her mother made for her, being unable to afford anything store-bought. As a result, Molly's mother loved clothes. Since her husband balked at her requests for money to buy new ones, she took a job in a boutique. She spent almost everything she earned on new outfits, showing them off to Molly before hiding them away in the back of her closet. Two weeks later, she told Molly, she'd bring the outfits out of hiding and put them on.

"That way, when your father asks me if an outfit is new, I can say that I've had it for a while," she confided.

Molly came to me for help getting a handle on her spending. She could not seem to deny herself anything – but she had almost nothing set aside for her future. Although she earned a good wage, she spent it all on credit card bills. Having rejected what she saw as her father's stinginess (that's what her mother called it), she'd gone to the other extreme, not even comprehending where her money went.

"I work hard and deserve to treat myself." This was the money story Molly told herself. In fact, she was overcompensating for her fear of feeling deprived – a fear that she soon conquered with a monthly budget and a commitment to stick to it.

Fear of the Unknown

Who gave you your first lessons about money? If you're female, you may have learned from your mother, who may have had a household allowance to budget and conserve money – if you learned anything at all. If you're male, you are more likely to have learned the importance of earning money as well as growing it with wise investments.

In our culture, boys are encouraged to take risks with money and "invest" and create a "business." Sadly, many women still view being good with money as "masculine and aggressive."

Thankfully, because of Title IX of the Federal Education Amendments of 1972, which prohibits discrimination based on gender in federally-funded educational institutions, girls and women have had the opportunity to compete both athletically and in the classroom. Sports, especially, teaches competitors how to apply themselves, work with others, and to win and lose gracefully. These skills are important in business and, certainly, when dealing with money. More younger women are competing better in the money game.

Things are changing, but at an evolutionary pace: one generation at a time. Many women still haven't a clue about how to manage their finances. And we all know about "fear of the unknown," the great shackler keeping us from learning, growing, and living our best lives.

If you're reading this book, you probably realize at least on some level that money fears are holding you back. But in Western culture, being afraid of anything is seen as weakness, so we may tend to push our fears away – perhaps into what the great psychologist Carl Jung called the "shadow." This is the side of ourselves whose existence we don't want to admit, even to ourselves. The shadow is where our darkest impulses abide, only to surface when – surprise! – we're looking the other way. To change this paradigm, we need only decide and act. A single tiny step can take us in a new direction – from a fearful scarcity mentality to a joyous, self-loving abundance mindset.

Shining Light on the Shadow

Have you ever eaten an entire pint of ice cream in one sitting? That could be the shadow self acting out. If you have a tendency to overeat and you haven't faced it head-on, it will compel you to dig in when your defenses are down – when you're feeling stressed or lonely, for instance.

Many people have money fears dwelling in their shadows. Fear of feeling deprived might lead to overspending. Fear of ending up destitute – a very common fear among women – can cause tight-fistedness and even greed.

Instead of letting our shadow tendencies control us, Jung wrote, we need to take control of them. To conquer your money fears and embrace money, instead, as a tool for self-love, you must not only face those fears, but get to know them intimately.

A therapist I know once likened the aspects of the shadow self to the story of King Arthur and the knights at his round table. To ensure the loyalty of all his knights as well as his control of them, King Arthur maintained close relationships with each. Not to do so could have dire consequences.

Love > Fear

This book is about facing your money fears, bringing them out of the shadow and into the light where you can really see them. It's about not only controlling those fears, but transforming them into something beautiful – into love, of money and, especially, of yourself.

"Perfect love casts out fear." Once you've courageously looked your money fears in the eye, you can start to feel compassion for yourself. You can embrace your fears, and even feel love for money as a glorious, empowering, life-affirming friend, a tool for achieving your best life.

You don't need to *make* this happen. Follow the eight steps I'll reveal in this book and your money fears will transform themselves. The answer already lies within you: All you need to do is open your eyes.

"Man's mind, stretched to a new idea, never goes back to its original dimension," Oliver Wendell Holmes wrote. No woman's mind, either.

Instead of being fearful or intimidated by money, what if you embarked on a journey to money love? What if you stretched your mind to accommodate not fear, but possibility?

How I Know This Works

My eight-step approach to changing your financial future really works. In more than thirty years as a Certified Financial Planner, I've guided many people on the path away from fear and led them to a secure, free, joyous, and peaceful money life. I've also learned so much in my own life, not only as a professional, but as an athlete, entrepreneur, mother, wife, friend – and survivor. I've dealt with a crushing, life-changing accident, struggled with infertility and dark nights without hope, and, like so many of you, a painful divorce.

We are not so different, you and I – no matter your income. In fact, you don't need a lot of money to walk this path and achieve great results. You only need curiosity, courage, determination, and the commitment to devote a few minutes a day to working through the exercises I present here. They'll help you reflect on your economic perspectives and take simple, clear actions to rewire your behavior and achieve a healthier, happier life.

From Fear to Love: Eight Steps

This book comprises eight chapters, each designed to take you one step closer to financial freedom. These steps apply to every person, whether you work a minimum-wage job or head your own successful company.

Along the way, I'll talk about my own hardships and how these concepts helped me endure them. I'll also share stories from my three decades as a financial advisor to inspire you as well as show how each step works in practice.

Walk with me, and I'll help you:

- Gain **clarity** and **focus** by examining your stories and goals
- Unlock your **patterns**
- Change your **mindset**
- Continually **transform your goals** over time
- Become **supremely confident** – with money and, as a result, in yourself.
- Develop a **purpose** that's more important than money
- Set your **intentions** mindfully and follow them
- Chart the course for your **personal journey** using money to help you get there
- Live your **best life**, whatever that means to you

The Steps

Curiosity:

"Curiosity will conquer fear even more than bravery will," wrote the Irish writer James Stephens. Indeed, to study our lives and motivations with curiosity, open to whatever we might learn, requires a special kind of courage. Facing a foe in battle might be less frightening!

Does the idea of financial freedom excite you, in spite of any fear you might be feeling now?

Are you ready to make a change?

Why? What inspires you to want to take this step? Did something specific happen – a life event, a conversation?

Prepare for this chapter by writing it down in your Love Money Journal – the notebook or computer file you'll keep solely to reflect and document your journey with me. Write down as many details as you can think of, in list or narrative form, describing what you heard, saw, smelled, tasted, and felt.

Was this a new experience, or has it happened before?

What did you learn about yourself?

"Experience is the teacher of all things," Julius Caesar said. Learning from our experiences is the essence of wisdom, and it begins with evaluating our past, learning from it, and allowing it to guide our future.

Self-Empathy

Feeling down on yourself because of your spending habits, poor organization, lack of a budget, or something else? Give yourself a break. It's easy to get bogged down by our perceived inadequacies or past failures, so extend some grace to yourself with this next exercise. Ready?

Take a minute to write down eight money mistakes. Then, list one action to take toward correcting each of these mistakes. Think about how you felt before, during, and after each of these actions.

Finish this step up by posting your list of solutions somewhere you'll see it regularly, maybe on a Post-It note in your bathroom, bedroom, or closet.

Be kind to yourself if you stumble. Transformation only happens overnight in fairy tales. Changing behaviors is a step-by-step process – remind yourself of this and congratulate yourself for getting started!

Organization

Where's the clutter in your life? Most of us have it somewhere: in our closets, our basements, even in the knick-knacks on our shelves. And then there's money clutter – all the things we spend our money on that we don't need, won't use, and, sometimes, don't even really want.

The problem with clutter comes down to that old "you can't see the forest for the trees" analogy. Clutter obscures our view of what we're looking for – in this case, money clarity.

Do you have clear priorities for your money? Do you know what your needs are as opposed to your wants?

Spending on the things we want is perfectly fine – I'm not an austerity maven, in case you haven't figured that out. But if you want to change your spending ways and even save some of your income for that proverbial rainy day – unforeseen medical bills, a need to take time off from work, a family emergency, or, simply, a decision to retire – you'll need to prioritize.

Start by making two lists: one for "must have" expenses and one for those you "want to have." Since we're working with that lovely infinity-symbol 8, try to include at least eight items on each list. This is your chance to dream a little as well as to get to know yourself better. Is dining out a "want" or a "need?" What about gift giving? Manicures and pedicures? Do you *really* need to color your hair, or to have a professional do it?

This exercise can be extremely helpful as you move into the Organization chapter. Taking the time to clearly define what you need versus what you want will help you prioritize what is truly important to you. Want to take things a bit further? Devise a spending strategy, breaking your spending into three categories: "Living," "Saving," and "Loving."

Organizing your finances is an essential part of organizing your life (something else we'll discuss in chapter 3). But, like taking the weekend to clean out your basement, it can also be an act of discovery. Search your soul as you make your lists. Dare to dream. And – have fun!

Charting Your Course

Have you ever taken a road trip to someplace new without using a map? Probably not. It's rather difficult to reach your destination if you don't know which roads to take.

The same holds true for your money-fear-to-money-love journey. For success, you need to know where you're going. "It's not the destination that counts, but the journey" is only partly true. Driving around aimlessly can be fun for a while – but if you're going nowhere, that's where you'll end up.

To avoid life in the breakdown lane, you'll want to set some goals. Get out your Love Money Journal, sharpen your pencil, and start writing: What are your financial goals for the next eight weeks? Where do you want to be one year from now? Three years? Five years? Eight? Why are these goals important to you?

Add It Up: Taking Inventory

Do you know what you have, what it's worth, and how much you owe? Figuring out your assets and debts – which, combined, add up to your net worth – can be a bit intimidating. If you've never done it before, it's a real eye-opener.

It's also a necessary step on your Money-Fear-to-Money-Love journey. Knowing your starting point is at least as important as knowing your destination, no?

In this step, you'll make a list of everything you own that has worth, that you could sell quickly. Don't include personal items like clothing or jewelry.

Limit your list to things that have tangible value, such as cars and other vehicles, real estate, perhaps a business that you own. When listing their value, consider how much you could sell it for today, not what you paid for it and not what it will be worth in the future.

Ready, Set, Go!

Now that you've laid the groundwork, you're ready to embark on your great adventure. This chapter is where your money goals intersect with your life goals. How can your money help you live your best life?

In this chapter, I'll provide practical tips for how to meet your goals, including sticking to your budget and living within your means as well as saving for items and experiences you want instead of going into debt to buy them.

And because life has a way of throwing curveballs, I'll help you establish and build your emergency fund, which allows you to pay in full for unexpected events such as a car breakdown or a medical emergency instead of going into debt. Then you'll need a plan to replenish this fund by paying yourself back. Why would you treat yourself less respectfully than you would treat your bank?

Commitment

Any good relationship requires commitment – including, and especially, your relationship with yourself.

Do you have a life partner? If so, you may want to encourage them to work through the steps in this book with you. Discussing your goals and dreams together can strengthen your bonds and enable you to support each other when old habits rear their heads.

But even if you're not partnered, commitment is still important. A daily practice of journaling your thoughts, fears, and dreams, envisioning the future you want, reading this book, checking your budget status and/or investments, or something else will help you make money-mindedness a habit, which increases your chance of success.

This chapter will help you improve communication with your partner about finances, provide options for organizing money in a two-income household, and challenge you to identify, together, what you value in your relationship. If you're single, it will help you strengthen your personal commitment to a joyous financial future - the ultimate act of self-care.

Self-Actualizing

"Being the change you wish to see in the world" applies not only to the public realm, but also to your financial life. In this chapter, you'll get to imagine not the worst that could happen – the approach of so many financial advisors and a sure path to defeat, in my opinion – but the best.

What if you had no scarcity of money, but only abundance?

What if all your basic needs were taken care of? How would you feel knowing that?

What if you could fulfill your dreams without any consequences – no bills, no worries, no struggles (from a money standpoint, at least) – but joy?

What if you had the knowledge and skills you need to organize and create experiences in life according to your desires?

Having your money work for you is essential and empowering. Write down how you would feel to have choices and options, and the means to choose what's best for you and your life.

All You Need Is Money-Love

Changing your money-fear into money-love – not the greedy kind (this comes from fear), but the use of money as a life-enriching tool – won't be as simple as making up your mind to do it. To switch your money mindset from fear to love requires intention and action.

Love, it's said, is a verb: it's something we do. By the same token, money can become an instrument of love when you use it with love. To get there, you need curiosity, which entails an open heart as well as an open mind. You need clarity. You need a plan. And you need to want that peace of mind that well-managed finances can bring.

Maybe this all feels like an uphill battle – but I promise you that *you can do it.* You have what it takes to reach that summit. I will be with you every step of the way, supporting and encouraging you, and reminding you that *you are worth it.*

You are worth the time it takes to complete the exercises in this book. You are worth discovering, deeply knowing, and freeing – enjoying the freedom that comes from tearing up your self-limiting stories and rewriting your scripts.

Come with me. Let's use perfect love to cast out fear so you can live your best life. With this book and your own intelligence and imagination to guide you, you're about to discover a wonderful truth: that the best, for you, is yet to come.

Chapter 1

CURIOSITY

"Curiosity will conquer fear even more than bravery will."
~James Stephens

Your first step from fear to love is this: You need to get curious about yourself and your money habits.

"Is that all?" you may ask. Indeed, getting curious sounds like fun – even easy, to some.

In truth, curiosity can be treacherous. Ever hear the term, "Curiosity killed the cat?" It means *be careful what you look for.*

Humans are complex creatures. We learnt at an early age to present a facade to the rest of the world and even, often, to ourselves. Scratch the surface of that calm, or smiling, or confident person and you'll likely find someone different – and not just one different person, but many. Not all are nice, or nice-looking. Some may even be monstrous.

You may be tempted to look away, but I encourage you not to. Or, if you must avert your gaze, make sure to bring it back. Until you've come face-to-face with *all* your aspects, you can't love them, or yourself. Chances are, peering into that dark mirror will frighten you, but not nearly as much as you fear your unknown self – and the awesome powers within you – now.

Like children afraid of the dark, we all fear the unknown. How well do you know yourself?

Ask yourself:

- What are your monthly bills?

- How much do you spend on non-essentials, and why?

- Does money "burn a hole in your pocket" to be spent?

- Do you squirrel it away and deprive yourself?

- Do you give your hard-earned money to other people in your life – even those who might not deserve it?

- Are you an impulse shopper?

- Do you bargain-hunt, or do you save up for nice things?

- How much are you saving every month?

- And, following every answer to these questions comes perhaps the most important one: Why?

Self-knowledge is the key to self-love, and all the lovely things that go with it: Joy. Power. Freedom. The great love of your life. The fulfillment of your most cherished and heartfelt desires. But before the knowing comes the seeking, and before the seeking comes … curiosity.

Curiouser and Curiouser

'Curiouser and curiouser!' cried Alice (she was so much surprised,
that for the moment she quite forgot how to speak good English);
'now I'm opening out like the largest telescope that ever was!'
~Lewis Carroll

If there's one quality that defines the daring protagonist of Lewis Carroll's *Alice in Wonderland*, it's curiosity. Alice plunged down rabbit hole, nibbled wafers and mushrooms, joined impromptu tea parties and croquet games (risking her head in the process), and much more, driven by her insatiable curiosity. For her reward, she had an unforgettable adventure – and, no doubt, learned some things about herself, like how sensible and courageous she could be.

The same is true of Dorothy, the inimitable heroine of L. Frank Baum's *The Wizard of Oz*. Who can ever forget the moment she steps out of her drab existence and into the world "over the rainbow" in vivid technicolor? She encounters little green Munchkins, a good fairy, a wicked queen, flying monkeys, a wizard, and more – and makes three lifelong friends, including a lion who trembles at the slightest sound. Who would *you* rather be: bold, curious Dorothy or the timid Cowardly Lion?

These characters stick with us because they teach us what it means to face our fears, and dare to forge ahead on the magical, sometimes terrifying, path that is our lives.

In the introduction to this book, I invited you to approach this chapter by writing down the conversation, or event, or feeling that inspired you to read this book and work on yourself. If you haven't done so, grab your notebook and write it down now. What inspired you?

One of my clients confided in me that she was motivated by a conversation she had with *me* over lunch. "You warned me that I was one medical event from losing everything," she said. "I didn't sleep all night."

That was tough love, but it worked. At that time, just a few years ago when she was in her late fifties, she had almost no money set aside for her future. Now, at sixty, she's into six figures, and adding to three investment funds every month. At her current rate, she'll reach her $1 million goal when she's seventy-five – and have her house paid off, too.

"I wish I had met you ten years ago," she said recently. "I would have been so much farther along than I am today." I encouraged her to think of her journey this way: She is so much farther along today than she was before, and on her way to financial independence! It is *never* too late to start.

Open Your Eyes, and Look at the Day

Old habits can be like old, worn-out shoes: they may feel comfortable, but they won't take us very far. Patterns of behavior, too, can keep us where we are rather than giving us the support we need to venture on new paths.

This book was written during a global shutdown, when depression and anxiety served as constant companions to many. Others lived in denial. All three states are static: depression inhibits motivation and desire (and curiosity), anxiety fills our mind with negative, counterproductive thoughts and emotions (such as fear), and denial blinds us to what is really happening, preventing us from seeing what needs to change.

Breaking out of these patterns is extremely difficult. It may feel impossible. But I'm here to tell you that you can do it! I know from personal experience that we can do *anything* we set our minds to.

I lived in denial for quite some time, myself in a bad marriage that I'd convinced myself I couldn't leave because of our four young children – two sets of twins, three boys and a girl all less than five years old. I'd tried for years, even undergoing fertility treatments, to finally conceive. Five years later, I was miserable with my husband, but resigned to grinning and bearing it for the sake of the kids. I threw myself into my role as "mom" and into my work as a financial advisor with a large company.

Then, during a business trip in New York City, a speeding SUV slammed into me as I crossed the street. The impact shattered my pelvis into more than forty pieces. Recovery was a slow, painful process involving reconstructive surgery. I might never walk again, the doctor told me. Running? Forget it. I, a competitive triathlete, had run my last race.

The experience broke me wide open. I felt devastated to hear the grim prognosis, and to imagine spending life in a wheelchair instead of walking my boys to school when they began kindergarten in the fall. It seemed so unreal that I couldn't believe what the doctor said.

But he also told me something else: ninety-eight percent of a patient's outcome depends on their mindset. The realization streamed into my broken-open self like a golden beam piercing the dark: *I* was in charge of my future – no one else.

The Locus of Control

In 1954, psychologist Julian Rotter came up with the concept known as the *locus of control*. People who think they have control over their lives tend to be more accomplished, he found. On the other hand, those who perceive that outside forces are calling the shots often achieve less.

It's easy to see why: if what happens in life is out of our hands, what's the use in striving? What's more, feeling out of control can exacerbate the depression, anxiety, and denial that can hold us back from meaningful change.

On the other hand, trust in yourself can be a great motivator. I can attest to that. After hearing my doctor's report, I cried. After all my efforts to become a parent, now I wouldn't be able to play with my children, let alone walk them to school. I'd never ride a bicycle again, never go swimming, never again see the world from the top of a mountain.

But a part of me still didn't believe his predictions. I'd been a strong, successful, *powerful* person before my accident. Had that changed? As I lay in my bed, I began to think about all that I had achieved in life, and all I wanted to accomplish. I could do anything I set my mind to, I decided. I *would* walk my boys to school. I *would* run, and ride a bicycle, and play with my children. I felt my own determination rise within me, and I told myself, "You've got this."

Broken Open

I'm not giving you "when life give you lemons, make lemonade" optimism. This story is real – it happened to me. Or, I should say, except for the accident, I *made* it happen – all of it. Nobody and nothing could stand in the way of my achieving what mattered to me. This tends to be true when our goals spring from an emotional state. Those who didn't support me – such as my husband – I eventually cast aside. And when autumn arrived, I walked those boys to kindergarten – after working tirelessly with physical therapists to reach that milestone. To be able to make that journey alone, on crutches that morning, was such a big moment.

When life breaks you open, look inside yourself and see who you find. Get curious!

Your life isn't going as you'd envisioned? Welcome to the club. There's a reason for the saying, "Life is what happens while you're making other plans." But giving up on your goals and dreams isn't the answer – that's letting outside forces control you. As Dr. Rotter discovered, it leads to nowhere.

Blaming others isn't the way, either. To do so is to admit that you aren't in charge of your situation. Besides, blame is often a cover-up that hides your fear, which can be the one thing standing between the life you have and the life you want.

What's Your Excuse?

It's easier to make excuses than to examine yourself. You have no retirement savings because you've never made much money? I often hear this from expensively dressed women with professionally-styled hair and nails.

We all make choices every day. Do you choose to invest in your future rather than spending on the here-and-now? If you're not earning enough, might you learn a new skill?

Do you soothe yourself with shopping therapy? Putting money into a savings or investment account can feel just as good. Do you know how much you'd have today if you'd set aside ten dollars a week starting when you were eighteen?

You've never had time to learn the markets or to read up on financial planning, or even to make a budget? The hour a day you spend on social media – or half that – could definitely be put to better use.

Not taking responsibility for our choices leads us down a dead-end road – or, more fitting, a cul-de-sac, where we circle around and around ourselves, never learning anything and never getting ahead.

As a financial planner these past thirty years, I've heard my share of excuses. I've probably heard them all, in fact. And the reason for every excuse comes down to fear.

Get curious: Take out your notebook and write down one area of your life that you know you could improve but haven't. Then write down every excuse you can think of for why you haven't done it.

Here some of my favorites:

1. **The 'victim' excuse:** "It's not my fault." The victim rationalizes their lack of progress and blames someone or something else for not reaching their goals.

2. **The "Who care?" excuse:** "It won't make a difference no matter what I do, so why even try?"

3. **The "I don't have time" excuse:** "I want to take action as soon as I do this other thing." And when it's done, something else comes up. The next thing you know, you're out of time.

4. **The "We've always done it this way" excuse:** "I've never been able to do it in the past, and there's no reason to think I can do it now or in the future."

5. **The 'rulebook' excuse:** You've got rules in your head that you think you cannot break. For example, your rulebook might say that investing money is not something that women can or should do. "It's just not how things work."

6. **The "I've had enough" excuse:** You've already done enough and you're fed up. You're not going to put in any more effort. Whatever you've done up to now will have to be enough (even if it isn't).

Stop the excuses! Do you see how, in making them, you are abdicating control? It's time to take charge of your life.

Get curious: Take out that notebook. Studies have shown that, if we describe our goals in writing, we're much more likely to achieve them.

Write down your problem (or goal) and how you have been avoiding it. What fears have kept you from living the life you want?

To fire up your goal-setting session, try these strategies:

- **Be realistic.** Get clear with your "why." Why do you want to achieve your goals? Why are these goals important to you?

- **Be courageous.** Dare to dream. Stretch yourself by asking, "What would I do if I knew I couldn't fail? What would bring the most joy and happiness to my life?"

- **Choose powerful words.** While describing your goals, use engaging, powerful words that evoke an emotional reaction – "goal chaser," "dreamer," "achiever," "hard worker," etc. What inspires you, and gets you excited to wake up in the morning?

- **Set up reminders.** Place your written goals or reminders of them where you'll be sure to see them, such as on a mirror or fridge. Keeping your goals at the forefront of your consciousness makes it more likely that you'll accomplish them.

When you approach your fears with curiosity, you can explore and get to know them. Your understanding will allow you to defuse your fear and you can take control and finally create a life that aligns with your goals and values.

Rewrite Your Script

Now is the time to see your situation with a fresh perspective. If you build strategies that allow you to refocus or re-assert yourself, you'll be better positioned to take advantage of opportunities that come your way.

If you could do so, how might you re-shape your life? What would you do differently? What new path would you create for yourself?

Change can be so hard. Wherever we find ourselves in life, we're most likely there because of a series of choices that we made. Each decision has built on the next, and to alter our course may feel treacherous. What if we fail? That's a big one. And I say, what if you do fail? Didn't Thomas Edison say that, in inventing the light bulb, he hadn't failed one thousand times, but that to succeed took one thousand steps?

If you pivot to a new place in life and you don't like it there, you can usually pivot back. The worst that could happen probably isn't going to. If you quit that job you dislike and take the one you want or go to school to study your passion and you regret the change, you can get a new job. There's always another job, right?

An All-Too-Common Scenario

Some changes, yes, are irreversible.

Maybe what breaks you open is that someone close to you dies, or you divorce. Maybe your husband (probably not your wife) managed your joint finances without including you. Now, when he's gone, you have no idea what you have and what you owe, what you can spend and what you shouldn't.

As strange as this scenario might seem in the twenty-first century, unequal relationships still exist. They're more common in older marriages, but I see plenty of younger women leaving it to their husbands to earn and invest the money that supports them and their households.

I met one such woman recently. Her eighty-year-old husband had died, leaving her with the kinds of surprises none of us wants to experience at any time, especially at sixty-five. She'd known he liked to take risks but hadn't expected to find that he'd taken second and third mortgages on their enormous house that cost $45,000 a year just to maintain. Those loans had funded their lavish lifestyle, but it was all smoke and mirrors: their income didn't pay the costs. He left her the debt-ridden house and an income of just $35,000 per year. She's now facing bankruptcy and considering getting a job – and ruing that she didn't involve herself in their finances.

As Warren Buffet famously said, "When the tide goes out, you see who is swimming naked."

"Money is masculine," women say to me. If they're taught anything, it's to budget and spend wisely the income that, they sense, belongs to their husbands – after all, he earned it. Too often, though, they don't even get to handle the budgets or bill paying. Their husbands give them an allowance that they must make last until the next installment.

And when he dies or they divorce, the woman has little or no idea about familial bank accounts, insurance, investments, or debts.

This is hardly surprising when you consider how little women talk about money. Even today, when so many women are primary breadwinners supporting their families or themselves, we shy away from discussing our pay, our financial goals, our investments, and so on. Our patriarchal culture has taught us that it's crude to talk about money.

We'll explore relationship dynamics and money in depth in chapter 7, *Love and Money*. For now, suffice it to say that the woman who turns over the finances to her husband also hands him the power in the relationship. How can she get her share of that power? For starters, she can get curious.

How Did You Get Here?

Women, in particular, have fears regarding money. Many of us worry about becoming homeless. In many cases, this fear is irrational. Perhaps because we saw our mothers and grandmothers working to stretch the household allowance their husbands gave them as frugally as they could, we've inherited a "scarcity mentality" regarding money. This phenomenon, often a fallacy, tricks us into thinking that there's a limited supply. In response, we can become grasping, even greedy, anxious to get our share – or fearing that, at any moment, we might run out.

When it comes to money, these fears may affect you no matter what your financial state. If you struggle to make ends meet, you may fear not having enough money. If you have enough to pay your bills, you may worry about having enough for the future. If you have plenty of money, you may fear losing it all—that your investments will plummet or that you will lose your job.

But there is no scarcity of money! On the contrary, it's in abundant supply. How much more relaxed would we feel if we accepted this fact? Then we might see money as a tool, and exercise full control over how we use it. Even if we tend to spend impulsively, giving in to those urges is a choice. Why fear something you own? Unless that is, you don't have control of your money. In which case, it's time to change that paradigm.

Get curious: Write down your current thoughts and feelings regarding money and answer these questions. Follow each answer with an explanation as to why you answered as you did.

- Do you feel anxious about having enough money?

- Do you feel out of control with spending, or maybe too controlled?

- How did your upbringing affect your money mindset? Were your parents successful at saving money, or were they constantly in debt?

- Which lessons, consciously taught or not, did you learn about money management from your parents?

- Who were your money role models during your younger years? Many parents would agree that they were not good ones. But finances are not usually taught in schools. How else could we learn about saving, spending, credit, bills, etc. except at home?

- Which person (or persons) do you strive to emulate financially? What about them do you admire?

- Do you fear money? How can you change that feeling into ones of trust and love? How can you use money as a tool to help you succeed in your goals?

The Elephant in the Room

Curiosity is more about questions than answers. But how can we get answers about a topic that women are convinced is taboo?

Do you know your women friends' annual incomes? Their debts? How much they have invested, and where? If you're a woman, do you and your female friends and colleagues discuss your money fears and anxieties, or even your triumphs?

Even my own mom won't tell me, her financial planner daughter, certain things about her financial life because she's too embarrassed. She doesn't feel comfortable. She struggles with self-esteem.

If any of this sounds like you, you may be surprised to find that women investors are reaping better returns than are men, according to Forbes by Fidelity Research 3/30/2021.

"It demonstrates that women are great investors, and when they take action, it can work out quite well for them," Lorna Kapusta, head of women investors and customer engagement at Fidelity Investments, told CNBC.

Do you link your finances to your sense of self? (We'll discuss this more in chapter 2, "Self-Love.") So many people do, especially in a capitalist society. When you earn or save a healthy amount and feel good about yourself because of it, this is healthy. But those who don't or can't or aren't quite sure tend to worry that they might get judged for their lack of money. This is one reason for our collective reluctance to discuss our finances.

But the proscription on money talk isn't just personal. It's cultural. Why, you might ask, would the culture try to suppress the sharing of this kind of information? One reason might be this: the fewer who understand money, the fewer will possess it. Although there's certainly not a scarcity of money, there is a finite amount of it – and those who have the bulk of it (men) just might want to keep it for themselves. Money is power, after all.

There's a reason why we're discouraged from comparing notes about pay with our male colleagues. Check out these startling findings from the American Association of University Women (AAUW):

- Women working full time in the U.S. are paid 83% of what men earn. At the current rate of change, we won't achieve pay equality until 2093.

- In terms of overall wealth, a single woman has only 32 cents for each dollar a single man has. And the wealth gap is even wider for women of color, who have just pennies for every dollar a white male has.

One of my clients was shocked to find that her male colleagues with an identical title to hers, but far less experience and talent, earned a higher wage than she. Her female manager revealed the findings of an internal survey she'd done and advocated for my client to get a raise. Why did it take this kind of advocacy to right the situation? Because the woman had never asked her male colleagues what they were making.

We'll talk about almost anything else but money. How strange is that? Even with our own sexual partners, the subject is regarded as too personal. That's right. In our society, talking about money is more intimate than bumping uglies. Why is it that people are so often more willing to get physically naked than fiscally naked?

If we approach money with curiosity, we can remove the stigma attached to talking about it or, by extension, thinking about it. The more we know, the better we can grow. And because money is so intimate, the first place to look is inside ourselves – not with judgment, but with curiosity.

Know Thyself — and Become Powerful

The only real power each of us has is choice. What do you choose to think? What do you wish to focus on daily? What one small step can you take to move yourself closer to your dreams?

By taking even simple steps, you can start moving from nothing toward abundance. With intention, you can move from competing to cooperation.

Focus on what brings you joy. You are not a victim of your circumstances. Instead of saying things are happening *to* you, say things are happening *for* you. Challenges are a gift. Trials allow you to shake up your reality and realize that you are so much more than a person just trying to survive another day, only to do it all again tomorrow.

You are a conscious, deliberate creator of your future.

Not only is it possible to live the life of your dreams, but it is also possible for YOU. One of the worst things a person can do is to live a life unfulfilled. And if you get to the life of your dreams and you still aren't happy, guess what? You can change your dreams.

"We see time and again when women do get more engaged and ensure their money is invested to achieve what's important to them, their stress levels go down. When women know their money is working as hard as they do – that's goodness and helps them feel better about their future," Kapusta says.

Money Fears Are Real. What Are Yours?

Do you feel anxious when you sit down to check your finances? A lot of people do.

You look at your bank balance, and a sinking feeling hits the pit of your stomach. Where has all the money gone? Other emotions kick in when you check your accounts: guilt perhaps, or even shame—especially if you spend on impulse.

It's no wonder you dread dealing with money or even fear it.

Fear of money is a common enough phenomenon, but you can overcome it much more quickly than you might think. I'm not referring to chrematophobia, an extreme fear that can extend to even touching money. I'm talking about the garden-variety fear, the kind that causes us to freeze up or even avoid considering how much we're spending until it's too late.

Dealing with this aversion is crucial to your financial future, no matter what your situation is now. To start, I suggest exploring your relationship with money.

Get curious: Now that you've explored your formative influences on your money mindset and habits, let's look at where you are today.

- What problems or issues do you face concerning money?

- Do you have trouble controlling your spending impulses?

40

- Do you give to everyone except yourself?

- Do you understand that money is supposed to serve you, and not the other way around?

- Have you ever asked for help with your money?

- What in your life is most valuable to you?

- What do you have to give? How much, for you, is enough money—I call this "enoughness"—and how can you put yourself there?

Pondering these questions with curiosity – and following up with "why" – will help you conquer your fear of money and lead you to a more fulfilling life.

Look Your Fears in the Eye

To gain control of your finances and conquer your fear of money, you've got to face your fears head-on and take the drama out of the story you have around it. Here are some tips:

Check your bank accounts daily. "Exposure therapy" is a technique often used to help people overcome their phobias—and it works. By forcing yourself to look at your bank account every day, you will stop dreading surprises because there *won't be any*. It might be challenging to do at first as you confront your spending choices, but the repeated exposure should quickly make it easier for you to monitor your accounts.

Pay yourself first. A healthy savings account can make you feel less like you're walking the high wire without a net. Set up an automatic deposit of X amount of money (say 10% of every paycheck) to routinely go into your savings account, removing the temptation to skip the month's contribution. The amount does not need to be large, only consistent. Try it! Chances are, you won't even miss the money.

Cut your costs. What is the one thing in your weekly expenses that you could do without? That daily coffee on your way to work? The tanning package? Restaurant lunches? Even those tiny amounts, saved instead of spent, can add up.

Check your successes and failures. What expenses have you succeeded in eliminating? Which savings techniques have worked for you, and which failed? What did your parents do, money-wise, that you would want to emulate, and which of their mistakes would you like to avoid? You can learn valuable lessons from your own experiences and those close to you.

Work on your credit score. To get a loan from a reputable lender, you may need a score of at least 700. If yours is low, work on paying off your debts.

Sell off your "extras." Which items do you have that you no longer need? Do you have a closet full of unworn clothes or electronics you don't use anymore? Consider selling them, either in secondhand shops or over the internet, on sites such as eBay, Amazon, or Craigslist. Turn your old junk into profit.

Recycle. Reduce-Reuse-Recycle is more than just a catchy slogan. Sustainability helps you, your finances, and our planet.

- **Cultivate an "abundance" mindset.** I've saved the best for last. Feeling grateful for what we have is the first step toward true abundance. When we take our money for granted, it tends to slip through our fingers unnoticed. When we truly appreciate it, we tend to use it more wisely. "You need to empty the cup to fill it back up." Have you ever heard this phrase?

That fear of emptiness can lead us to try to fill our lives indiscriminately, perhaps even with purchases we don't need. Anxiety can also cause us to avoid paying attention to our finances. What if our accounts are empty?

Try turning this fear into possibility: an empty account, like an empty cup, is just waiting to be filled. "Perfect love casts out fear." Loving yourself, and appreciating what you have, is a positive step toward abundance. Appreciation cultivates a wealth mindset—not because it magically brings more money, but because it will make you want to take better care of what you have.

Someday, you may find that your cup is not only filled but running over. That's abundance—something not to fear but to celebrate.

Tapping into Your Inner Baddass

A while ago, I created the Baddass Babes, a social media community that has nothing to do with financial advising. I spend so much of my life keeping track of markets, maintaining relationships with my clients, and helping people pave the way to their financial future – but there's another side to me.

My Baddass side.

By day, I am a financial advisor. But I am also a mother, passionate athlete (yes, a former rower, skier, and yes, I compete in triathlons), and strong, fiery woman who has created a business from the ground up.

I wasn't merely handed opportunities as a young entrepreneur. I acted on the belief that I could make a better life for myself and my family. Sure, I'd had setbacks and failures; at times, I've been tempted to throw in the towel and give up. Over the years, though, I've learned to treat delays as learning experiences and challenges as opportunities to grow.

My Baddass Babes community was a way for me to connect with women and help empower them to chase their best lives. I like to say, "We are Baddass Babes: so bad, we need an extra D."

Success doesn't happen overnight. Progress isn't linear. The first step toward harnessing your inner baddass is to acknowledge your problem areas.

We all have that shameful, tiny voice in our head that says, "You could be doing *this* better." For some people, it's taking care of their finances. For others, it's staying physically active, eating healthy, or achieving more in their career.

Whatever your problem may be, there is a self-defeating tactic lying within that problem. To make positive change, you need to own your problems and discover how you allow it to defeat you, and why.

Rewrite Your Script

So much of life happens because of the stories we tell ourselves. What stories are keeping you from using your money in ways that enrich and empower you?

Luck isn't something that happens, but something we create. Look at Jeff Bezos, the founder of Amazon and one of the richest men in the world. He started as a book reseller who saw, and seized, an opportunity to sell to schools and universities. As time went on, he expanded his business to include sales of other items. To succeed, he took many changes, and kept his online marketplace on the cutting edge of technology. You might look at his lavish lifestyle and think he's lucky – but I think he's a person who has seized the opportunities that came his way and created many others.

Do you ever resent the rich? What good is that attitude doing for you? Why not get curious, instead, and learn how they made their fortunes? You might learn something new about the world, or about yourself. You might feel inspired to write, then rewrite, your own money story.

Try these simple exercises to understand your money stories so you can rewrite them, break your bad habits, and start down the path of financial freedom.

1. **Describe your relationship to/with money.** Do you feel comfortable talking about money, or is it a topic you avoid? Why? Understanding your personal history will help you uncover some of your obstacles to effectively dealing with money.

2. **Ponder your money mistakes.** This can be a hard thing to do, given the feelings, as mentioned earlier, of guilt and shame that may arise. But we learn best from our own mistakes, and to paraphrase the famous quote, a person who doesn't learn from their mistakes is bound to repeat them.

3. Why do you make the mistakes you do? Where did you learn these behaviors? As a child, you may not have learned how to differentiate between "wants" and "needs," and spend or save accordingly. As an adult, you have the opportunity to teach yourself.

4. **Explore what money means to you.** What pleased you as a child? Did any of these things involve money? Chances are,

most of them did not. Think back to those times, tapping into that innocent joy, and remember what you knew as a kid: many of the best things in life are free. What brings you joy?

"Money makes the world go around," from the 1960s musical "Cabaret," is a truism that's also true. If you want the world to turn your way, you've got to take the wheel. That means overcoming your fear of money so you can take control of your finances. Once you've given yourself permission to be curious and examined your relationship with money, then you can start transforming it—joyously—from dreaded adversary to lifelong friend.

Chapter 2

SELF-EMPATHY

*"Learning to love yourself may be the most difficult step on your
money-fear-to-money-love journey,
but it's also the most important."*
~Unknown

When you've had a rough day, what do you do to rid yourself of the bad feelings? I used to go shopping.

I'm sure we've all done it: headed to the mall or the boutiques and bought things we didn't need, just to get that serotonin hit. It feels so good to try on new clothes and imagine the fun we'll have wearing them, or to browse fancy kitchen stores thinking of the amazing meals we could make with this gadget or that, or redecorate our living room or bedroom with new furniture, carpets, curtains, or art.

Maybe it's not things that cheer you up, but experiences. A day at the spa, or an extravagant meal out? Why not? An impromptu trip to somewhere exotic? Sure!

"This," we think, "is self-love. I'm taking care of myself with this purchase." But are we, really? If we've budgeted for our expenditures or saved for them, we can perhaps say "yes" with confidence. But if we're spending money we don't have, the price we'll pay is, ultimately, much greater than we'd bargained for. And, like coming off a drug- or alcohol-induced high, we'll likely feel worse after our binge than we did before we started it.

Unlike conventional therapy, "retail therapy" works only in the short term. Whether it's the realization after the endorphins have subsided or the bills that hit us at month's end, instant gratification proves again and again to be no kind of self-love at all. What's loving about saddling ourselves with debt or, over the long term, even bankruptcy? What's nurturing about stressing ourselves out?

Have you ever known adventure seekers who live in their van? I knew a successful businessman who lived in an almost-empty house because he spent so much of his income on his skydiving obsession, craving the adrenaline rush that followed every jump. Living the literal high life, he forgot to set aside money for retirement. "I live in the moment," he'd say, saying he preferred to spend his money on experiences over things.

Eventually, however, his practice fell – due to his heavy drinking, no doubt – and he found himself unable to afford his precious hobby. He continued to skydive, anyway, charging his numerous weekend jumps to his credit cards. When he began having health problems, he found himself unable to pay all the medical bills, and lost his car and his house. At last, destitute, he filed bankruptcy.

By not planning for tomorrow, was this man practicing self-love or self-neglect? The highs he experienced may have soothed his soul in the short term, but they cost him dearly in the long run. Instead of security, he found insecurity. Instead of contentment, he suffered incredible anxiety.

All We Need Is (Self) Love

When we do anything that harms us, no matter how wonderful we feel at the time, we're not loving ourselves. To understand what is and isn't self-love, think of a child, parent, or someone else whom you hold dear. What would you wish for them? Money anxieties? Bankruptcy? A lifetime of working with no opportunity to retire or even slow down?

"Treat others the way you want to be treated" is a maxim in our culture. I would add, "And treat yourself the way you want those you love to treat themselves." Aren't you at least as deserving as they are?

Giving to others, in fact, can be a wonderful way to give to ourselves. When one woman I know is feeling blue, she volunteers at the local food bank. As for me, instead of shopping for new clothes, I'm better served by going to my closet, picking out three items I don't wear as often as I used to, and giving them away to a charity or friend.

Try it: you may experience, as I do, a rush of joy that's at least as satisfying as the thrill of shopping for yourself – perhaps even more so. I think our ancestral heritage as hunter-gathers may be an underlying cause of the urge to "gather" items in shopping sprees, and that gathering items even from our own closets can help satisfy this impulse. Doing for others can be so uplifting, and without the gut-wrenching bill afterward.

Researchers have found, in fact, that giving to others produces a "high" that's longer lasting than the joy we feel from receiving. This applies, in my experience, whether we're giving to others or giving to ourselves – as opposed to taking from ourselves, as we do when we spend impulsively.

Self-Love Starts with Self-Empathy

I've been doing something new lately: asking myself every morning, "What will I do to love myself today?"

Love is a verb; it's something we do, not just a feeling. I like how this morning ritual not only reminds me of the importance of self-care, but that it also challenges me to take action toward achieving my goal. Perhaps I'll pay a bill, set aside money into my savings account, or send a thank-you card.

Yes, paying bills is self-love! It feels good to take care of yourself financially. I know people who don't even open their bills, thinking on some level that what they don't know can't hurt them. This is how credit ratings get destroyed, and life choices taken away. This happens especially often with credit card bills. If they stress you out, here's an easy answer: don't use your credit cards. Save for what you want, instead.

In this age of instant everything we call the internet, saving seems to have gone out of style. How many people who've bought Tesla cars or trucks had the money for that purchase? Banks make it incredibly easy nowadays to get a loan, and why not? They earn income on every dollar we borrow.

And when we want something we see online, it's so easy to click "purchase." Increasingly, retail sites even offer us a payment plan with zero down. Once again, they aren't doing this out of the goodness of their hearts – they want your money, plus interest. And if you can't make the payments on time, your credit rating could be ruined.

Home equity lines of credit are another great example. Often, banks open this line based on the equity you have in your home, with an adjustable interest rate. I've seen people use this account for all kinds of expenses, driven by a "fear of missing out," or FOMO. But if interest rates go up, so does your payment, and the total amount you owe. If your payments become more than you can afford, you may be forced to sell your house at a time when it's not advantageous to do so. How about fear of missing out on the chance to get the best price for your home?

"Buy now, pay later" may sound good, but here's a better approach: "Pay yourself now, buy later." Imagine saving up for that trip you want to take and having the money in the bank before you go. How joyful you might feel before, during, and after the journey, instead of anxiously trying to pay off your credit cards or loan after you return. Giving yourself this kind of life is truly self-loving.

It's time to get off the debt treadmill. You end up running as fast as you can but going nowhere.

One of my cars – the car I keep at a second home – is a Honda Pilot held together, in part, by duct tape. People often express astonishment when I arrive somewhere in this car. They expect the CEO of her own financial company to jet around in something flashy and new. If I were more concerned about looking successful than being successful, I might do so – but to me, a car is just a means of transportation, not a status symbol.

We can put on "airs" for others all day and night. It's easier to do now than ever before: we even have photo filters that can make us look slimmer and more attractive. Why do we need to alter ourselves? Aren't we good enough as we are?

Here's a secret: your worth as a human has nothing to do with your appearance (although society has long – too long – valued women for beauty) or the appearance of having a high net worth. Having a high net worth, on the other hand, can have a *lot* to do with your sense of self-worth.

Love Yourself, and Money Will Follow

People often confuse the two: net worth and self-worth. Have you ever thought, "If I had this amount of money in the bank, I would feel as if I made it?" What does that number represent to you?

Ask yourself if you suffer from this kind of self-talk:

- "If I had this many friends and people who adored me, then I would feel as if I made it?"
- "If I lose weight, I will be worthy of love."
- "That boob job will make me feel more worthy."
- "I need that newest computer/phone/car/clothing to feel better."

My wealthiest clients are also stealthy. They don't spend ostentatiously but live in the same modest home they've occupied for decades. They're not out to impress anyone because they are secure in themselves, lovingly treating themselves to strong relationships with family, friends, and community. Rather than buying a second home, taking fancy European vacations, or driving flashy cars, they use their money to support charities, education, and the arts.

They value education for the next generation; they care deeply about their families, especially their grandchildren. They don't need to impress anyone to get the love they want, because they already have the love they need.

"The problem with love is that it's not for sale," famed business tycoon Warren Buffett once said. "It's very irritating if you have a lot of money. You'd like to think you could write a check: I'll buy a million dollars' worth of love. But it doesn't work that way. The more you give love away, the more you get."

Do you spend time trying to impress people you don't even know and probably don't care about?

Your net worth or even your number of social media "followers" does not equal your self-worth. It is critical to make that distinction.

Your net worth is a simple number that can be calculated on a balance sheet. Self-worth, however, is a lot more complicated. Those with low self-worth may think the way to increase it is to work harder, put in more hours at the office, and accumulate assets and others' admiration.

"Money can't buy me love," the Beatles sang. "Money can't buy happiness" is a time-worn adage. Both are true. If you value possessions (or experiences) over people, you're headed for emotional bankruptcy. Even completing all the exercises in this book won't leave you better off than before. Because a person with low self-worth can never be fulfilled.

All the money in the world won't boost your self-esteem. Your financial goals met, you might feel the glow of success and the hormonal rush that accompanies it, but once those feelings ebb, you'll just look for another external source.

People who love themselves don't need to seek eternal sources of validation or affirmation: they have all they need within. How did they get it? Perhaps their parents nurtured it in them; in that case, they'd be among the fortunate few. Most of us must, instead, cultivate our sense of self-worth on our own, or with others' help.

As Buffet notes, no bank account exists where self-worth debits and credits can be transacted. Self-worth can't be traded on the New York Stock Exchange, nor does it have a number to indicate your significance. However, you can open your own personal self-worth account and make deposits, increasing your self-love in increments, because *you* are in control.

Here's a secret: genuinely successful people who have both high self-worth and net worth did what made them successful not for the money but for the love of whatever it is they did. They enjoyed the process, and still do, not setting their sights on their bank accounts, primarily, but instead on the lessons they learned, especially from the mistakes they make.

"Success is not final," Winston Churchill said. "Failure is not fatal. It is the courage to continue that counts."

Know Thyself

Hollywood fantasies aside, you can't really love someone until you know them. The same holds true for loving yourself. And the first step toward self-love is to take a good look in your inner mirror. Maybe you've done this work, but have you scrutinized your relationship with money, warts and all?

Do your finances keep you up at night? Is living paycheck-to-paycheck causing you to spend out of fear and desperation, not with intention? Have you considered taking out a payday loan or dipping into your retirement just to make ends meet? Do you wonder how to keep the wolves – creditors – from knocking on your door?

To identify when and how you process money-related stress, check in with your body the next time you feel discomfort over a bill or some other financial matter. What triggered the response? How does it manifest itself physically? Is your stomach clenched? Does your head hurt? Do you feel tension in your neck or shoulders? Are you gritting or grinding your teeth? Do you feel the urge to turn away or even to run?

You're experiencing money stress – and it *is* taking a toll on your physical health.

Now: Imagine *not* feeling this stress. When bills arrive, you're calm, knowing they're taken care of. That shopping spree or spa visit you take yourself on brings only good feelings, because it's in your budget. When you travel, you know how much you can spend, and you have the money already set aside. And should something unexpected occur, you're unflappable – because you have enough in your emergency fund to cover it, and a plan to replenish any funds you have to use.

Money and managing personal finances are top life stressors in America. Thirty percent of Americans say they are "constantly worried about money." It doesn't have to be so.

We can control so few things in our lives: how we relate to money is one. Getting control of ourselves in this relationship not only can help us to live more secure and productive lives, but we also get more peace of mind. Saving for retirement and saving ahead for the items and experiences we want to purchase gives us more financial independence and lets us enjoy life more.

Treat Yourself to Healthy Boundaries

If your financial habits have spiraled out of control, being self-critical isn't the solution. Take responsibility, yes, but also, forgive yourself. The way you've used money is tied up in so many variables: how you were raised, your values, marital and family status, salary or wage, and your ability to set and maintain healthy boundaries. Self-boundaries can be the most difficult to enforce. We are masters at making excuses and rationalizing.

A woman in her early fifties came to me for help. She had almost nothing in her retirement savings account and wanted to change that. She had a big pile of debt and struggled to make her mortgage payments – yet she dressed in expensive clothes and traveled extensively.

Looking over her statements, I saw that she'd received a $1,200 COVID-19 stimulus check from the U.S. government. What had she done with it? She'd flown to Florida with a group of friends!

Poor boundaries can manifest on more micro levels as well. What if, say, your friends want you to join them for lunch, but your budget for dining out is tapped?

"I need friend time," you might tell yourself. "I can go just this once and make up the difference next month." But will you?

Why not enforce the budget you've put in place for yourself? You could try asking your friends to go for a walk, or meet for a picnic, or invite them to your place.

"I'm sorry, but it's not in my budget." Practice saying this. And make sure to congratulate yourself every time you do say it. There's no shame in taking care of yourself; indeed, it's something to celebrate. By using the word "budget," you can help break down the stigma of using that "forbidden" word among your friends.

Love yourself: For a self-loving approach to your financial future, "Think globally; act locally" is a great motto. Dare to dream big: reach for the stars and give yourself permission to get there one small step at a time. Here's how:

1. **Set financial goals.** Be realistic, honest, and strict, giving each goal a timeline with measurable steps along the way. Define precisely how you will achieve your goals, including what you will do and when. These steps can be small or large, depending on your circumstances and desires. Just having a plan is what matters: **the difference between a dream and a goal is a plan.** And you may find that just this one act gives you greater peace of mind.

2. **Feel *all* the feels.** Once you have a clear vision of your goals, ask yourself, "Why do these goals matter to me?" Let yourself feel each reply, all the way to your toes. What would it feel like to pay off those student loans? How much cash would you free up each month if you weren't making that car payment or mortgage payment – and how would that feel? What if you added money each month to your retirement account? How would you feel knowing that it's there, and growing? How would having an emergency fund affect your state of mind? Tying your goals to emotions helps your brain remember those associations. Then, when you need to recall your goals in the future, your mind will have them ready to use. Think big; shoot for the stars. You can do anything you put your mind to if you're willing to work to make it happen.

3. **Be honest with yourself.** Pull up your statements and make a list of what you have and what you now owe. Separate what you *must pay* each month and which expenses you can cut or even eliminate. Now is the perfect time to work "on" your life instead of "in" your life. This step might not seem like much fun, but the aim here isn't to chastise or deprive you: it's to enable you to enjoy your money. If you're worried that a medical emergency or needing to go into long-term care as an elderly person

will wipe out your savings, consider buying long-term care insurance. Then you can move through life with confidence that your money exists to serve you, not the other way around.

4. **Define your values.** What's important to you? What is your mission in life? Some people want a nice home. Others value experiences such as traveling. Some cherish the notion of leaving something behind for their offspring.

5. **Learn from your mistakes.** Don't beat yourself up – love yourself! We've all made money mistakes, and we'll probably all make more of them. What matters is whether we correct our errors where we can and learn from them.

One of my clients had to file bankruptcy seven years ago because of credit card debt. She still uses her cards, but pays them off every month, even when it hurts. Recently, she began budgeting for her credit-card spending to avoid surprises at billing time. She's taking one step at a time toward financial independence. Think of your gaffes as being part of your education, forgive yourself for making them, and move on with your new plans. If you slip again, get back up and keep going. Always remember that you are not alone. Many, many people are in the same situation as you!

6. **Stay on the sunny side.** Did you know that, according to research, we can't be simultaneously stressed and thankful? For our brains, it's one or the other. Which would you rather feel? A positive outlook can go a long way toward keeping you focused on your goals. Again, shifting your mindset is a matter of making small changes. Consider talking and thinking about what's working well in your life, as opposed to focusing on what isn't going well. Limit your exposure to the news – many outlets present negative news or sensationalism to keep us clicking or to hold our attention through their revenue-generating ads. If you do feel stressed about money or anything else, try taking a walk. Get out into nature, if you can, this is a proven stress-buster. While you're out there (or even if you're just sitting on your sofa), practice gratitude. Ponder all the good things that life has given you and express how thankful you are. Even just being alive is a blessing!

   Staying positive is essential to successfully making any life change. Negativity and feeling guilty will kill your drive. Instead, acknowledge your small victories; celebrate them and be grateful for every step you take toward reaching your goals. Money is a bit like good health; having it doesn't guarantee happiness, but not worrying about it makes life a lot easier.

Change Your Money Mindset

You may think that the only way to become wealthy is to work extremely hard, or be in the "right" career, or inherit from a rich relative. Or maybe you think it's out of your control. But these thoughts aren't reality: they're in your head. They come from a "fixed" money mindset that stands between you and financial independence. The good news is you can change them!

In all my years as a financial advisor, I've found that the number-one factor determining the quality of your financial life is your mindset about money.

In her groundbreaking psychology book *Mindset,* Dr. Carol S. Dweck outlines two ways of thinking that help determine our success in life.

'Those with a "fixed" mindset tend to think that we, and our circumstances, are set in stone, and that we really can't change much. These are the people who say, "But it's always been done this way."

People with a "growth" mindset believe that anything is possible and that we can become and do whatever we set our minds to.

Guess which mindset increases your chances of success?

The world's wealthiest people have a "growth" money mindset. They're open to learning about finance and investing as well as discovering new opportunities and trends, and they embrace the idea of growing their money, as well. They don't overthink or over feel it: they realize that money is a neutral tool, one of many tools at our behest to improve our lives and communities.

Money is no monster to be feared or avoided. There's no shame in having it – or in not having it. So why do we fear it?

Maybe you come from a low-income family. It's hard to imagine yourself as well-to-do because you have no role models for that. Maybe you've heard wealthy people derided as dishonest or exploitative, and so you think having money would sully your character. Maybe you're a creative person with a fixed money mindset that says earning a good living at what you love requires you to "sell out." Maybe you were taught by religion or other beliefs that giving is virtuous, especially if it causes you to suffer.

Do you ever self-sabotage when it comes to money, by spending more than you earn, giving your money to those who don't deserve it, telling yourself you can't afford to set anything aside for the future, or performing some other self-defeating act?

Are your money beliefs holding you back from building your own empire? Do you feel doomed to struggle because you were born into a lower-income family?

Most people aren't even aware of the self-defeating scripts that run on a constant loop in their minds. Most people have instinctual, non-supportive, fear-based beliefs about money, wealth, and success influenced by parents, friends, teachers, the media, and the Internet and social media.

But you have the power to change your mindset. Your beliefs are not laws, or unbreakable rules. If a belief isn't not serving you, you can simply replace it with one that does. You can shift your perspective, too, from one of "scarcity" to one of "abundance." But first, you need to shift your mindset about yourself.

Instead of, "I'm not worthy," you need to tell yourself, "I'm worthy of these experiences. I'm worthy of having my house paid off. I'm worthy of being able to cut back on my work hours so I can spend more time doing things I love." You need to speak to yourself from a loving, supportive place, which entails ridding yourself of unsupportive beliefs,

Love yourself: Complete these sentences:

Money is _____. (Fill in the blank)

Money means for me _____. (Fill in the blank)

Then, fill in the blanks to discover what beliefs are holding you back:

I am not financially free because _____.

I'd love to have more money, but _____.

As you fill in these answers, other limiting or dysfunctional money beliefs may arise. Write them out, then reframe them into more positive and supportive affirmations. Here's help:

DYSFUNCTIONAL BELIEF: I am simply not good with money and never will be.

REFRAME IT: Anyone can learn to handle their money. I use my knowledge about money every day.

DYSFUNCTIONAL BELIEF: Money is the root of all evil.

REFRAME IT: Money is a neutral tool that we can use to further good or evil intentions. It is my responsibility to make the most of what I have, and to use it according to my values.

DYSFUNCTIONAL BELIEF: Money can't buy me happiness.

REFRAME IT: Money gives me the freedom to do things that improve the quality of my life.

DYSFUNCTIONAL BELIEF: I never have any extra money.

REFRAME IT: I choose to manage my money wisely because more money comes my way when I do.

DYSFUNCTIONAL BELIEF: I can either make lots of money or do what I love, but I can't do both.

REFRAME IT: I don't have to choose between making money and pursuing my passion. I can do both!

DYSFUNCTIONAL BELIEF: The rich get richer, and the poor get poorer.

REFRAME IT: My financial future is entirely up to me. I already have within me everything I need to create financial abundance.

DYSFUNCTIONAL BELIEF: I've reached the level of wealth I wanted; the hard work is behind me, and now everything will be great.

REFRAME IT: Life is a joyous and never-ending design project, and I can't wait for my next adventure!

As you reframe your own "fixed" or negative money beliefs, you may be surprised by how your mindset changes, too. You may see financial opportunities you'd never noticed before. The power of positive thinking is mighty, and so are you for listening to, loving, and honoring yourself. Change your mind and you can change your future, which is also true about your relationship with money.

Your beliefs truly shape your outcomes. Don't be a passive participant in your own life. By actively reframing the things that are holding you back, you can design the life you deserve – and that includes your finances.

Remember: this book, and the work you are doing, are *not* about having money. Riches and wealth are not the same. Being rich means having money. Being wealthy means having the time and freedom to live the life you have always wanted to live,

Shopping 'Therapy': Buy Now, Pay (Big) Later

Do you ever wonder why you think you need more? There is a reason why it's called "Shopping Therapy." It's easy to get a dopamine boost from the process of buying things. It's a short-term fix of an excitement bubble that will always get burst when the bills come rolling in. It is why casinos are full of people looking for a dopamine hit of feel-good hormones.

What a rush it can be to "treat" yourself when you've been feeling blue. A new outfit, the latest computing gadget, something for the house, and *voila*, your cares blow away like dust on the calm wind.

Science shows that indulging the urge to "shop 'til you drop" does lift one's spirits. Just the anticipation of acquiring something new triggers the release of dopamine, a neurotransmitter that controls our brains' pleasure and reward centers.

Why does "retail therapy" work as it does? Theories abound:

- **It helps us transition.** "Suddenly singles" (newly divorced or separated couples) can surely appreciate the "out with the old, in with the new" attitude that can spur or justify purchases of clothes, home furnishings, and other items that we may not need.

- **It boosts confidence.** Who doesn't feel better wearing a new outfit?

- **It provides an escape.** Shopping takes us out of our problems for a while, at least, and gives us something to look forward to—purchasing and then using our acquisitions.

- **It makes us feel worthwhile.** As humans we provide for our homes and family and take care of ourselves.

- **It connects us with others.** Shopping puts us close to friends, neighbors, and others in the stores and malls and on the sidewalks.

But as so often happens with "instant gratification" activities, retail therapy demands more than just the price at the register. The surge of good feelings quickly ends once we've attained our desired object and receive the bill. Realizing what we could have done with that money, instead, may mire us in regret—making us feel worse than before.

Some people think their things define them. Some of them have strong emotional connections to the memory of how they got that item or perhaps an experience they had in the presence of that item. Those emotions can keep them tethered to those things, and in some cases, people hoard physical stuff to help keep them feeling safe. Be aware of the reality that will hit when you have to pay off the credit card purchase. Was it worth it?

When we are on our own, the fact is that the responsibility to take care of ourselves rests solely on our shoulders. We must think not only about the present but about the future, as well. The good news is, money can be our ally—if we use it wisely.

So—how to achieve that feel-good "rush" without sabotaging your future? Here are some tips:

- **Take a list.** Write down the things you do need and shop for those items only. Dopamine will still flood your brain as you shop, but you're less likely to regret your "spree" later.

- **Pay with cash.** It imposes limits on your spending, so you won't have to deprive yourself of something else later. Also, you won't have to suffer the hangover of a credit card bill.

- **Shop your closet.** It costs nothing but can be just as rewarding. Maybe you'll find that dress you haven't worn in so long, and you'd forgotten. Put it on, and it may even feel like you're wearing something new. Anything you don't want, you can give away—providing a dopamine hit, helping your community, and even providing you with a deduction at tax time.

We all get the blues from time to time. There's nothing wrong with wanting the "quick fix" a shopping spree can provide. Engaged consciously and with the goal of proper self-care, retail therapy can give a much-needed boost during a difficult time. Rather than sabotage your financial future, consider shopping in a way that enhances it. You are worth it!

Chapter 3

ORGANIZATION

"For every minute spent in organizing, an hour is earned."
~Benjamin Franklin

This chapter is where things get real – where you put your newly curious and self-empathetic mindset to work to establish the foundational building blocks for your financial success.

You've already been asking yourself the questions that will help you set goals and devise a budget; you've (hopefully) come to understand how putting up boundaries around your spending is an act of self-love. The third step on your money-fear-to-money-love journey is organization, which starts with putting systems in place to help you meet your goals.

The very idea of a "system" may sound complicated, even intimidating. Truly, it's not as bad as all that. We use systems all the time to organize our daily lives. The clock and the twenty-four-hour day are human-designed systems established to help us track time; the calendar, too, gives us a common framework for planning our lives.

Our jobs have systems, and so do our workplaces. Policies, procedures, software, and ad-hoc systems keep the wheels of business turning smoothly. My husband, an airline pilot, can fly a plane from any point in the world to the next, in sync and in tandem with other pilots with whom he may have never worked before. They can do the job together because they all know the standard operating procedures. We also have systems for getting up in the morning and going to work; for getting children to school and home again; for planning, shopping, and cooking meals; for managing the passwords of the apps and websites for which we have accounts; and much more.

In the business of your life, *you* are the CEO. It's incumbent upon you to make good decisions for your empire, which includes setting systems in place that help you accomplish your aims.

Many people, however, have no system at all for managing their finances. Throwing your bills in a drawer and forgetting them is not a system; it's a form of chaos. Systems impose order on chaos.

Your money system will help take the work out of achieving financial freedom, making it easier to realize your financial (and life) goals. Your system can remind you what to do, when to do it, and can even perform some tasks for you such as paying bills.

How you design your system is up to you. You can use a finance app such as Mint to track your income and spending; you can set up bill pay through your bank and schedule automatic payments; you can go the analog route and buy a numbered accordion file, then drop bills into the slots according to the date they are due. Maybe, as the book *Seven Habits of Highly Effective People* by Stephen R. Covey recommends, you opt to pay your bills as soon as they arrive: that's a system, too.

Money systems are important because they take the worry and guesswork out of managing your money life. They let you proactively manage your money rather than react to money shortages, debts, and financial emergencies. Having a system reduces your stress because it puts you in control of your money, one of the few aspects of life that you actually *can* control.

Clear Out the Clutter

When you organize your closets or cupboards or drawers or anything, chances are that you clear out clutter as part of the process. You discard items that you no longer need or like, or that maybe don't fit you any-more. You can do the same with your finances. It's actually a lot of fun to make room in your account for saving by getting rid of expenses that no longer serve you.

Here are some examples:

1. **Subscriptions.** How many apps, services, streaming sites, products do you pay for every month via subscriptions? How many of these do you actually use or need? I'll bet there are some you'd forgotten you had. The subscription

model, for many, is akin to the proverbial death-by-a-thousand-cuts. In many cases, paying as you go is less expensive. Why pay the monthly Amazon Prime fee to get free shipping if you only order a few items a year? Is it really worth the ten percent savings to get that facial cream every month when it takes two months for you to use up a jar? **Get organized:** Examine your credit card and bank accounts to see exactly what you're paying for, asking for each subscription: Do I need this? Do I use it? Would my life be worse without it? Then, go on an anti-shopping spree, canceling all the subscriptions that don't serve you.

2. **Freeze your credit card.** If credit card use is too great a temptation to resist, try freezing it – literally. Wrap your card or cards in a plastic bag, fill the bag with water, and place the package in the freezer. Then, when you want to charge something using your card, you'll have to wait for the ice to thaw. While you're waiting, you can ask yourself if you need the item.

This method won't work, by the way, if you've set up your credit card information to autofill for internet purchases on your laptop or mobile phone. If impulsive spending is your issue, consider removing these autofill options. When you decide to buy anything, just having to get your card from your wallet or from its frozen environs may give you time to talk yourself out of buying something that you don't really need.

Get organized: Check the payment options in your devices and, if you're an impulse spender, remove them. Then, put your credit cards and, if necessary, your debit cards, into the freezer.

3. **Set up automatic payments.** Credit card companies and banks routinely allow automatic payments – a feature of which you should take advantage, if you haven't already. If you need help, call your bank or credit card company and get someone on the phone to walk you through the process.

Get organized: Monitor your accounts daily to make sure you have enough money in them to cover your automatic payments.

4. **Pay off your debts.** Every dollar you're paying in interest could be going into your savings or investment accounts or spent on something fun. Put your debt on a timetable with monthly payments designed to pay off the highest-interest loan first, followed by the next-highest, and so on. Include this payment in your monthly budget and arrange for it to be paid via autopay, if possible.

5. **Build your emergency fund.** If you aren't already doing so, put some money away into a savings account or money market account to serve as an emergency fund. This fund, typically

comprising three to six months' expenses, gives you the cushion you need to feel secure in case something happens that's costly to fix: an accident, medical or dental problem, car repair, or home repair.

Get organized: Figure out how much you can set aside for emergencies – even $100 a month is fine – and start doing so, again using autopay if possible. If you need to dip into the fund, make sure to pay yourself back as quickly as you can.

6. **Streamline your budget.** Highlight every "must pay" item in your budget – your mortgage payment, for instance – and consider weeding out the excess. Do you frequently pay for dinners out? This is not only bad for your health – restaurant cooks add fat and salt to enhance flavors – but also for your budget. I enjoy fancy foods when I'm traveling and do splurge on nice meals then, but at home I cook (and love doing so), saving my money for those special trips.

7. **Streamline the rest of your life.** Decluttering isn't just a one-and-done activity, but a frame of mind. Clean out all your closets and sell the clothes to a second-hand store or donate them to charity. Clean out your drawers, your basement, your bookshelves. When you have too much stuff, it starts to own you, rather than the other way around.

The Joys of Material Minimalism

The Model A, the first car produced by the Ford Company, could travel up to only eighteen miles an hour when it was first introduced in 1903. That sounds slow today, but at the time it marked a major improvement over the horse and buggy.

By the 1930s, aerodynamics – streamlining – began to change automobile design, with an emphasis on speed. Even today, automakers offer light, sleek styles that slice through space and time with as little resistance as possible, faster and faster.

Streamlining your life can confer similar benefits. Do you feel weighed down by the burden of your too-large house, the boat you rarely take out, all the knick-knacks you must keep clean? How many of the records or CDs in your collection have you listened to in the past few years? When's the last time you used that hot tub, or played that big piano? How many cars do you really need?

Most of us know we own too much stuff. We feel the weight and burden of our clutter. And while we may want to simplify and have the clean, modern space of a Swedish interior design magazine, in reality, we spend way too much time and energy on maintaining our many possessions.

Having a lot of stuff can be detrimental to our health and well-being. Not only is owning more items increasingly stressful, but it takes a severe toll on our emotional happiness. I recommend purging what you don't need. Working towards developing a bright space can help you clear your head, save money, and build a peaceful and relaxing home life.

With most of our homes full of clutter and unwanted items, 13.5 million households – nearly 11 percent – rent self-storage units. Most of these renters have basements or attics in their homes. The average cost of keeping all this extra stuff in a storage unit: $89 per month.

Many people utilize storage units as a transitional trapeze to get them from one point in life to another. Maybe they've moved from a house into a smaller condo, or have combined households with someone, or have inherited stuff from a family member. There were more than 49,000 storage unit facilities across the country – more than three times the number of Starbucks coffee shops! Think of how you could allocate $89 of your budget each month if you didn't have to pay that storage unit bill!

In fairness, pretty much everyone collects things. Reasons, according to the Guardian UK newspaper, include:

- Psychological comfort, for those who grew up feeling unloved

- Loyalty to a group, club, country, or sports team

- "Contagion" – the belief that the essence of the previous owner, usually a celebrity, could pass from the item to the new owner

- Existentialism – a desire to leave something of ourselves behind as a way to continue existing after we die

- Endowment – the feeling that something becomes more valuable to us when we own it

- Attraction – the desire to attract desirable mates by demonstrating our ability to accumulate resources

To this list I would add **insecurity**, which drives us to hoard items out of fear that we might need them someday or lose our ability to obtain more stuff; **nostalgia**, which is similar to contagion, but that causes us to keep things our loved ones once owned because they evoke memories or because we want to pass them on to the next generation; **status**, in which we see our possessions as impressive to others; and simply **not knowing** what to do with all the stuff we've accumulated in our lifetime.

I know a woman who sold her house and bought a small beachfront condo in Mexico. How liberating it was, she said, to be free of her stuff. But she isn't truly free of it at all. She rents a storage unit filled with items she can't bear to get rid of for fear that she might decide to move back to her hometown someday.

Even those without storage units may find their homes filled to the brim with unnecessary things, things that take money to display, and time and energy to clean, organize, and maintain. And yet, an empty home isn't tenable, either. We want to have a beautiful and comfortable space, and that requires beautiful, comfortable surroundings. Also, maybe you do play that piano; maybe you do need a second car. How can you find the balance between too much clutter and cultivating a space you love?

My friend Sue has moved more than seventeen times during the years I've known her. She and her husband enjoy buying houses, living in them for a while, and then selling them and moving on. I marvel at how she has done this so many times. One reason she can do so gracefully is that she regularly downsizes her stuff. Her system revolves around three simple rules:

1. Ask yourself if you have used an item in the last 12 months. If not, donate or get rid of it.

2. If you rarely use it, or if it is something that you can replace for less than $25, let it go.

3. If it is a family item you have inherited, ask yourself if your children would want it if you were to die. If not, let someone else find joy in it.

Get organized: Start your organizational purge. Go through your belongings one at a time and ask yourself the above questions. To get rid of the excess, sell your things, pass them to friends and family members, donate to charity, or toss.

Remember, choosing to tend to your personal space shows how you allocate your energy and time. Instead of using things to fill an emotional void or to buy love or happiness, start by clearing the energy and letting it go.

FOMO or MOJO?

Financially independent people tend not to overspend. Usually, they're quite frugal. Frugality is, in part, how they got to be financially independent. They save their spending for what's important.

Warren Buffet understands this principle. As CEO of the Berkshire Hathwaway conglomerate (comprising, among other businesses, Dairy Queen), Buffet had a net worth at the time of this writing of more than $115 billion. And yet he eats breakfast at McDonald's. He lives in the same house in Omaha, Nebraska, that he bought in 1958. He buys discounted cars and drives them until his daughter tells him, "It's getting embarrassing, Dad. Time to buy a new car."

Buffet's frugal habits are considered eccentric, but are they, really? To me, he appears to be supremely confident in himself. He doesn't worry about what others say. Nor does he have the "fear of missing out" (FOMO) that drives so many of us in America today.

What's happening on social media? Better check it out – you'd hate to miss something. We spend an average of two hours and twenty-five minutes a day scrolling, posting, and commenting on Facebook, Instagram, Twitter, and other social accounts. That's two-and-one-half hours in your day – more than fifteen hours a week, nearly the equivalent of a part-time job, that you can't get back. Think of all you could accomplish during that time. Maybe *that's* a better kind of FOMO.

We fear missing out on the latest news, the latest styles, the latest gossip, the latest opportunity to get noticed. We'll spend whatever it takes, timewise and money-wise for social approval, whether we can afford it or not.

Let's talk about facelifts. In 2016, 15.7 million people, mostly women, had cosmetic procedures done in the U.S. And the majority of them, I've read, earn less than $50,000 a year. Are these women spending their hard-earned cash in this way to endure the bruising, swelling, pain, and risks because they don't like the way they look, or do they do it because our culture values girls and women for physical beauty?

Don't get me wrong: I don't feel judgmental about any kind of "work" someone chooses to get done. Everyone should have a right to do as they please with their own body. The price is high, though, and I wonder if, in a culture that cherished women for intelligence and success – the traits for which we prize men – so many women would be willing to fork out $8,000-12,000 for a facelift.

Money is power, and these kinds of expenses drain the spender of both. FOMO is robbing us of our MOJO – our ability to take care of ourselves, to love ourselves, to give ourselves the life we have always wanted.

Often, the word "mojo" gets used as a slang term for "magic," but I also like to think of it as being short for "more joy." MOJO motivates us, and keeps us on the track for happiness by pursuing what matters the most to us.

Your joy can be your family, your career, your passion, or your talents. You know you are in the MOJO zone when what you are doing gives you energy, versus sucking the life and joy out of you.

So, how to let go of FOMO and cultivate MOJO?

1. **Limit your screen time.** Social media might be a quick fix, but as we've seen it drains away our time and even our self-esteem post by post, drip by drip. Just say "no" to Instagram, Facebook, Snapchat, or whatever the latest social app is that you tend to explore when you feel bored or lonely. Social media can start the comparison game; it looks like everyone else has everything you want. Commit, instead, to being in the present moment.

Write to yourself. Journaling is a beautiful way to reveal your emotions to yourself on paper. Try writing longhand instead of using a keyboard: Studies show that it has benefits for your brain. And journals are easier to keep hidden, and also easier to destroy if you so desire.

Let the Joneses be. Have you heard the phrase, "Keeping up with the Joneses?" The phrase refers to our endless striving to be like other people and have the things and experiences they have. It's a futile effort. If people aren't impressed by who and how you are, they're not going to change their view because you bought a nicer house or upgraded your wardrobe. That new handbag or car will not buy you happiness, but only a fleeting moment of joy quickly followed by surprise when the bill comes due. On the other hand, your self-esteem is worth more than all the money you can spend to fill that void. Why not build it up by saving for what you want? Paying cash is what will impress people, and if it's money you've saved, you'll also feel great about yourself.

Appreciate anticipation. Delayed gratification is underrated. You can find so much personal power by saving for a new item and paying cash for it (see above). "Buy now, pay later" might sound great, but the price is always high – in interest charges, in regret, in beating yourself up when you discover that another choice would have been wiser.

Trim the excess. Less is more. Get rid of the stuff. I highly recommend asking, "Is this item giving me joy or serving me in some way?" If not – even if it's Grandma's rocker, or a family heirloom – give it away or sell it. Someone else may need or cherish it.

Cultivate gratitude. Be thankful for what you have. Why do we always want something we don't have? The French psychologist Jacques Lacan said that a sense of lack underlies desire, which drives all humans. If you appreciate what you have as "enough," you won't need to spend money on acquiring new things: you can set it aside to fund your life's passion, instead.

Temerity, Not Austerity

I'm not suggesting that anyone live like a monk. I know I'm not interested in an austere life. I'm talking, instead, about temerity, defined as boldness, confidence, and courage – in other word, being "badass" enough to enact a system for making your financial freedom dreams come true. This is the essence of self-love.

This goal is long term, but you will find that organizing brings immediate benefits. If you want to feel freer of worries and hassle, lightening your load can be a great way to get there.

Material minimalism means living with intention. Rather than spending your days and nights amid items that either get in your way or just take up space, you'll shed the things that don't give you joy and keep only the things that do.

It means considering only your needs and wants, not others' opinions.

Do you live in that big house that takes all your time, energy, and money only to impress others? Consider downsizing.

Do you own an expensive new car because it's a status symbol? Why not sell it, buy a nice used car, and invest the difference?

Impressing others might be a lot less important if you realized how infrequently any of those people think about *you*.

Live within your means, and in time you'll have a lot more means. On the other hand, charging things you can't afford only traps you. Filling up your space with unused things fences you in. Living without a money system only sets you up to fail.

Learning to live with less, and on less, means you can spend more of your life doing the things you love rather than having to work all the time to pay the bills that your lavish lifestyle has racked up.

Your organized, system-driven financial life sets the stage for where you are now. So, where do you go from here? It's time to chart your course to financial freedom, goal by goal, milestone by milestone, rewarding yourself along the way. In the next chapter, we'll explore how.

Are You Ready for Financial Disaster?

In the financial world, many life events can be considered "disastrous." Hurricanes, floods, fires, or other natural disasters can devastate families and communities.

But what about different types of crises that can wipe you out financially? Small-but-mighty problems can be equally devastating, such as a broken water heater, sudden loss of a job, or an unexpected illness or injury. How prepared are you to handle a financial crisis?

Some forty-four percent of Americans say they could not pay an unexpected $400 expense out of pocket. They'd have to borrow or sell something to foot the cost.

Water heaters cost between $822 and $1,616 just to install – not including the price of the heater itself. Break a bone in the U.S. – the world's most expensive for health care – and you'll pay $34,500, *on average*, if you're not insured. Even with insurance, your bill will be a lot more than $400.

If you lose your job, unemployment benefits won't be as much as you earned by working, and they'll only last about six months. Hopefully you'll be able to find work before using up your benefits, but how will you pay your bills in the meantime?

We all know the importance of being ready for emergencies, but it's equally as important to be prepared for financial emergencies.

as well. How well stocked is your financial first-aid kit? It should include the following:

1. **An emergency fund:** "The time to repair the roof is when the sun is shining," and the time to set aside money for emergencies is when your finances are in good shape. A good rule is to save $1,000 immediately and then build your fund to three to six months' expenses. **Remember, the purpose of an emergency fund is not growth – it is your safety.** These are funds you access in the event of unemployment, emergency home repairs, or unexpected medical bills. When the emergency has passed, replenish this fund as quickly as you can.

2. **Insurance:** Having insurance reduces your risk of losing what you have if trouble should strike. Types to consider include:

    Life insurance – Having life insurance ensures that your financial dependents could pay off any significant bills or debts and live modestly if anything should happen to you.

    Auto insurance – It is important to review coverage, especially your "uninsured motorist" coverage. If you're in an auto accident or get hit by a car and it's the other person's fault, things could get expensive if that person has inadequate or no insurance. Uninsured motorist coverage can be a financial lifesaver, paying your expenses. I advise a high deductible, however. In the unlikely event that you will need it, it's better to pay the deductible from your emergency fund than to pay a higher premium over the months and years.

Disability coverage – Your most valuable asset may be your ability to earn a living. Do you have insurance to fill in any work gaps you might suffer in case you do break that bone?

3. **Cash on hand** – If a natural disaster strikes your area – increasingly likely in the age of climate change – you'll need some money on hand. Banks would likely be closed during an emergency of this type, and ATMs may run out of money or not function. Having cash on hand would allow you to pay for a hotel stay and food while you await repairs. I recommend you have at *least* $100 cash on hand, in small bills.

4. **A "Disaster Box"** – Place all your essential documents in a fireproof and waterproof safe or strongbox or, if they're digital, in a removable flash drive or external hard drive. These documents may include:

Household valuables identification: If your house burned down or were burglarized, would you be able to replace your valuables or get compensated for their loss? Take photos of everything or even a video to record your home's contents, making sure to open drawers and record what's in them, as well.

Medical information: (doctor's name, medical insurance ID and group numbers)

Valuable contacts: (lawyer, financial advisor, bank, insurance agent, etc.)

Financial information: (bank accounts, investment accounts)

Prescription information

Driver's license copy

Birth certificate

Social Security card

Insurance policies

5. **Beneficiaries:** Ensure that the recipients of your will, financial accounts, and trusts are accurate and updated to your current needs and wishes. You probably don't want your money going to your ex-spouse!

6. **Household preparedness plan:** Learn about emergency plans for your child's school, your workplace, and your neighborhood and surrounding community, and make sure that everyone living in your household also knows and understands the emergency plan.

Chapter 4

CHART YOUR COURSE

"Charting your own course isn't just more necessary than ever before. It's also much easier - and much more fun."
~Pink

Where do you want to go in life? This is an important question. If you don't know where you are going, you will end up somewhere else – perhaps where you don't want to be.

One of my clients is a published author. Her first book was a huge success, earning her hundreds of thousands of dollars. Thinking she had it "made," she spent her royalties with heady glee: picking up the tab for entire tables full of friends at restaurants, going on expensive trips, filling her wardrobe with designer clothes. Five years later, she wound up in bankruptcy because she hadn't devised a plan to take care of her money or herself – which are the same thing.

When we live without a money plan, we become like rudderless ships moving aimlessly through the waters, letting our passing fancies carry us like errant waves. This *laissez-faire* approach is like embarking on a road trip with no idea where you want to go or what route to take. Is this how you want to live your life?

If you feel intimidated by the idea of mapping your money journey, think of the task as simply writing a list. Do you make "to do" lists? How about grocery lists for when you go food shopping? Do you use recipes when preparing meals? These all define direction to arrive at a specific outcome.

Chart your course: Grab your journal and a pen and begin charting your course. What are your financial goals for the next eight weeks? Where do you want to be one year from now? Three years? Five years? Eight? Why are these goals important to you?

Think with Your Heart

Lists, like rules, were made to be broken, it's true. But if our end goal is truly important to us, we'll resist the temptation to take that side trip to nowhere, no matter what the brochures promise.

Emotion is key. The goals and tasks we feel strongly about – excited, joyful, even fearful or dreading – tend to stick in our memories longer. Neuroscience explains why by showing how goal setting works in our brains:

The area of your brain that forms emotions and motivation, the amygdala, evaluates your goal or task to decide how important it is. If it passes the "feel test," your frontal lobe gets involved.

Your frontal lobe dictates problem solving. It defines your direction: what, specifically, you must do to achieve your goal.

These two parts of your brain – your emotional and rational centers – work in tandem, often switching back and forth, to help you stay on your path toward achievement. This involves not only doing what you must to attain the result you want, but also avoiding situations that impede your progress.

Adding a "Why" to Your Try

For instance, if you have a goal to eat more healthful foods or lose weight but you feel fairly casual about it, then the next time you feel sad or lonely you might reach for the pint of ice cream in your freezer. Before you know it, you've eaten it all – and ultimately feel worse than before. That ice cream may have provided the quick fix you sought, but it didn't solve your problem, and in fact may have caused you to gain weight – the opposite of what you want.

But if you need to lose weight because your doctor has warned you that you're on the verge of developing a medical condition, the fear you felt when hearing the diagnosis may come back to you as you reach for the coveted container. You're more likely, then, to take only a taste of ice cream before putting it away, or to decide to exercise or meditate to make yourself feel better instead of consoling yourself with food.

Another example: maybe you're trying to save money because your parents told you saving was wise, but you don't have plans for the money in your account or any strong attachment to its use. When you go to the electronics store and realize that you *must* have a smart watch, you're more likely to spend some of your savings on that.

But if you're saving for a purpose, for instance, a house, and you've imagined yourself in it – entertaining friends on the front porch or in the yard, or putting in a beautiful garden, or having room indoors and out for your kids to roam – your amygdala may spring into action as you consider that expensive watch. The longing for a house and the associated images may overwhelm the urge to buy another electronic gadget. Your frontal lobe steps in to warn you that making this purchase will take you farther from your goal, making you more likely to stay the course and walk away with your savings intact.

Wise decision making involves a careful balance between reason and emotion. If you've tied a "why" to your goal and your reason has roots in an emotion, your frontal lobe is much more likely to help you reason away an emotion-driven, impulsive act. As you reach for the pint container or your credit card, it will try to steer you in a different direction. *Do you really need this? Is devouring this ice cream or buying this watch helping you to reach your goal or hindering you? Remember why you set the goal in the first place.*

You can also make this happen with conscious effort. When you find yourself doing what you know you shouldn't, stop for a moment. Take a breath. Ask yourself: what is triggering this impulse? Your rational brain will kick in, help you sort it out, and may even talk you out of it.

Stay the course: When emotions try to hijack your brain, they release cortisol, the stress-induced "fight or flight" hormone. Resisting these feelings is futile and may only increase your stress to the point of anxiety.

Instead of fighting your feelings in the moment or pushing them away, try sitting with them and letting them wash through you. Close your eyes, breathe, *feel* deeply. In twenty minutes or less your cortisol levels will have dropped to normal and you'll be able to think clearly again. If you need to take action in response to the stress, waiting twenty minutes can help keep you from making mistakes that you'd be sorry for later.

One of my clients was struggling financially but got caught up in a friend's plan to purchase a timeshare. When he came to me, he was despondent to be stuck with thirty years of monthly payments that he couldn't afford. It's too bad that he didn't talk to me first. I'd have advised him to give himself twenty-four hours before committing. Even twenty minutes might have made a difference.

Delaying Gratification in an Instant Culture

The Internet has turned us into a world of Veruca Salts – the spoiled-rich girl in *Charlie and the Chocolate Factory* – stamping our feet and demanding, "I want it NOW."

"Customer demands," businesses call it, and "demands" is right. Not long ago, people shopped for hours or even days to find a particular item. We'd spend the day driving or walking from store to store browsing the racks and shelves, touching fabrics, trying things on, savoring fragrances or flavors or the satisfying feeling of a fit. Now we do our shopping on a screen, purchase with a click, and expect what we buy to arrive on our doorstep the very next day. We not only expect instant gratification: we demand it.

Talk about a process that bypasses the cerebral cortex! When we shop online, it's amygdala all the way, baby. Freezing your credit and debit cards won't help in this scenario, not if your computer has the credentials stored and ready to use. Against the Internet's expediency, our rational minds don't stand a chance – and neither do our goals.

Or so we tell ourselves. But we are, ultimately, in control even of our digital spending, aren't we? We have the power to click away at any time, up until the moment of purchase. Of course, this may appear to be easier than it is. The real answer is to refuse to shop online at all, or only as a last resort – after we've exhausted our other options. If you're still struggling, try removing your card information from your device and logging out of your PayPal account. Then if you want to buy something online, you'll at least have to get your wallet, pull out your payment card, and type in the numbers. While you're doing so, your cerebral cortex may start whispering to you, reminding you of your financial goals.

Shopping in person offers other rewards, as well: the satisfaction you may feel at supporting local businesses and their owners; the joy of seeing friends unexpectedly in the same store; the knowledge that the clothes you've bought fit well and look good on you; the benefits to the planet – less packaging, no carbon footprint in the shipping, returns, and possibly a second shipment. And did you know that some large companies don't even repackage and sell the items their customers return? It's too expensive for them to do so, so they send those items to the landfill.

Dr. Laurie Santos, professor of psychology at Yale University, author, and host of the podcast Happiness Lab, suggests that savoring life's experiences can dramatically improve our happiness. Instead of mindlessly clicking and spending money that isn't in your budget, why not bring savorful experiences back to shopping?

Your new shopping system could look like this: You decide you want or need something, check your budget, and invite a friend or two to join you for a special day. Maybe you have money in your dining or entertainment budget to grab a glass of wine or cup of coffee together, adding to the fun. When you get home, you'll most likely feel happier and more relaxed, and you'll be able to enjoy what you bought on the very day that you purchased it. *That's* instant gratification!

Map your course: Using paper and colored pencils, draw yourself a map to financial freedom. It can look like anything you choose: curving and circling back or a straight line between you and where you want to go, with various milestones, pit stops, and pitfalls along the way. Keep your sense of humor as you draw pictures and dream up prizes to give yourself as rewards for staying on track, getting back on track, or reaching a milestone. Rewards don't have to be monetary: they could include a bicycle ride, a bubble bath, or a piece of your favorite chocolate.

Before you chart your course, however, it's important to establish exactly what "financial freedom" means to you. Does it mean retirement? Traveling whenever and wherever you want? Putting your grandkids through college? Being able to pass money and belongings to loved ones when you die?

The 6 "Fs" of Financial Freedom

Making lists can feel like the opposite of freedom—where's the spontaneity? But truly successful people know that to get what you want in life, you must first understand what you want.

Neuroscience supports this claim. Setting your intentions and creating a way to document your progress increases your chances of reaching your goals. Taking some time to dream, exploring possibilities, and getting to know yourself better can help you clarify your desires, set goals, and make plans for achieving them—and how to pay for them.

From buying a house to traveling the world to starting a family to retiring, the freedom to choose our best lives begins with financial freedom. As paradoxical as it may sound, budgeting, saving, and even cutting back on specific spending are often necessary to have the life you want.

To start, focus on the six "Fs" for financial freedom. Setting goals in each of these areas can help you see the big picture that is the arc of your life and create a map for where you want to be and how to get there.

Family:

If you are not part of a couple, do you want to be?

Is having children important?

If you already have a partner and/or children, what are your responsibilities to them as well as to your parents, siblings, and other family members?

Do you have grandkids, and do you want to save for their education?

Do your parents need care?

Do you want to leave a legacy? By the way – I don't suggest doing good for others by giving them money or possessions. You've heard the adage, "Give a person a fish and you've fed them for a day" right? The best way to invest in your loved ones is to help them to help themselves.

One of my client's children couldn't find a job after graduating from college and moved back in with her. My client insisted the child work if they wanted to live with her, and ultimately helped that child start a business – with a little money, yes, but a lot of wisdom, referrals, and cheerleading.

I've seen too many people sacrifice their own wellbeing for others' sake and adopt a self-defeating 'victim' mentality. But when we give our kids, siblings, or anyone else a blank check, we aren't their victim. The choices we make are our own. If anything, we're victimizing ourselves.

Friends:

Giving and receiving friendship is a core requirement for wellbeing. Good friends are worth their weight in gold. We need trusted people with whom we can share successes and joys, root and cheer for, and shore each other up through the bad times.

On the other hand, some relationships are toxic. These we must walk away from. If our "friends" don't lift us toward our higher purposes – this includes our financial goals – they aren't friends at all.

By the way, friendships don't have to cost a cent. Would you want a friendship based on material gifts? Giving a card – better yet, one that includes a personal letter – can be the most meaningful way to celebrate a special occasion or holiday. Chances are, they wouldn't use and don't need whatever you might give them, anyway. My mother is notorious in our family for re-gifting to us something we've given to her in the past. She doesn't need more things, she says. I still give her presents, but I make sure that each one is something I like – because I know I'm going to get it back.

Fitness:

This may seem a strange topic for a book about money, but you can't really enjoy life to its fullest if you aren't taking care of your body. Eating well and getting regular exercise – for me, daily – are a must. Having a fit and healthy body can increase your productivity, reduce stress and sick days, and give you the strength and inner balance to take care of others when they need you.

I'm not talking about joining a pricey gym or spending hours a day taking classes you don't like. A brisk thirty-minute walk can do wonders for your physical wellbeing. Why not make it a social activity and invite a friend to join you?

Play tennis or pickleball, ride your bike, put on the music and dance – do anything that you enjoy, and your brain and body will thank you for it. You'll be smarter and mentally quicker, your brain's release of dopamine will elevate your mood, and you'll be better equipped to think productive and positive thoughts to help you achieve your goal.

Not only does good health help you do better work and feel happier and more energetic, it also saves you money. In the United States, medical care costs a small fortune. Avoiding emergency room and hospital bills can help you become financially independent faster.

And don't forget mental fitness. What are you doing to take care of yourself mentally? A number of great meditation apps are available, some of them free, to help you learn mindfulness, positive thinking, and other mental-health-supporting practices.

Faith:

This "F" doesn't refer strictly to religious faith. To succeed in meeting your goals, you'll need to have faith in yourself, as well. But it helps to have a spiritual component when connecting our dreams and desires of today to a vision for our lives in the future.

Are you part of an organized religion? Attending services and other activities can help you connect with others of like mind and also revisit your purpose.

If that isn't your cup of tea, a simple five-minute meditation can reduce stress and help you focus. The key is to take some time every day to create calm and tap into your inner wisdom. Accessing this aspect of yourself makes it easier to connect with it when you need it, such as during difficult times. Making decisions made from a place of centeredness and groundedness helps ensure that you're not acting impulsively, but keeping your own wise counsel to do what's best for *you*.

Fun:

What do you love to do? Which activities consistently bring a smile to your face? Schedule in these activities on a regular basis.

Your brain needs the serotonin that pleasure releases so you can relax and feel motivated in other areas of your life. On the other hand, too much of a good thing can be counterproductive, decreasing enjoyment. Balance is critical. We have twenty-four hours in a day: why not devote eight to sleep, eight to work, and eight (or as close as possible) to pleasure?

Play is important for enjoying your life's journey. Skiing is great exercise, but it's also how I love to play. Doing anything in nature is pure joy for me. What do you love to do? Cook delicious, nutritious meals for friends? Dance with wild abandon to live music? Curl up with a cup of tea and a novel? Play with your children or grandchildren?

I once asked my grandmother, an amazing woman in her 90s with a master's degree in Latin, what she would like to have done differently in her life. "I would have taken more time to have fun on the way," she said. It's good advice – but I admit to having inherited her "type A" gene. I have difficulty taking time out for enjoyment and pleasure.

Field:

Work is at the top of many minds in our culture, and with good reason. "What do you do?" is one of the first questions we ask someone we've just met – and the answer has become synonymous with who we *are*.

If you're in a profession that you love, count your blessings. If it earns you an income that supports the other five "Fs," you are fortunate, indeed. (And if you don't love what you do or it doesn't support you, wise planning can change that.) I list "Field" last because too many see it as all-important and neglect the other essential aspects of life. Work is vital, but balance is everything.

If your profession isn't sustaining you or your other five "Fs," what to do? Maybe go back to school? Or perhaps you can figure out how to make the job you have more enjoyable or fulfilling.

Of course, no job is fun *all* the time. If it were, we wouldn't call it "work," right? Every day has challenges, and that's good. Solving problems boosts our self-confidence and can be satisfying in and of itself. There are times, however, when we feel stuck in a bad situation and can't find a way to make it better. At these times, we may decide to switch jobs or career paths altogether.

If your job isn't paying enough, can you advance to a higher-paying position at your workplace or earn more elsewhere? If not, perhaps you'll want to switch fields.

To start, consider putting in a few hours a week as a volunteer in the field that interests you, or getting a job in that sector. If you want to be a financial planner, perhaps find a job in a bank. If you've got your eye on becoming a doctor or nurse, work in a medical office. Getting the inside skinny on what your chosen career might look like can keep you from glamorizing it. Financial advising, for instance, requires a lot more than mere money savvy. It takes dedication, lots of reading and analysis, and a ton of organization. Ninety-eight percent of people who start their own financial planning businesses fail. Before you become one of them, do your homework.

Life is too magical, and too short, to waste. You can always accumulate more money and stuff, but you can't create more time. [Use the time you have wisely] – make it work for you, not the other way around.

They say that, when you think about a yellow car, you start to see yellow cars everywhere. If you spend more time thinking about how you want to spend your life, opportunities will come your way. Your thoughts have power – so why not spend more of your time doing what you love and loving what you do?

Picture Success — Literally

Once you've set your priorities and goals, create a vision board to help you visualize and realize your dreams.

Perhaps using a poster board as the base, paste on photos that represent your goals along with words of affirmation to support these goals. Then add a mind map with colors and other visuals. Place the board where you will see it every day—near your bed, perhaps, so you'll remember before going to sleep and when waking up what you want to achieve, and how to get there.

To know where you are going, you must first understand where you stand. Then you can choose your path consciously, avoiding distractions and pitfalls. When you stray from your goals, use your map to find your way back. Freedom to choose includes the freedom to stay on track and to reach your goals—which, to me, is freedom of the very best kind.

Get Out of Your Comfort Zone

It's easy to stay in your comfort zone; you're conditioned to do so. Change takes courage. Every neuron will react when you decide to do something different and start taking steps towards that new destination.

You are programmed to believe in the pattern of your past behaviors, but once you honor yourself and speak your truth, you have the option of doing better than you have ever done ever before. Your paradigms will shift.

To be the best version of yourself, you must always be open to change – and that includes getting your financial house in order.

Eight Steps to Financial Fitness

To move from fear of money (financial struggle) to love of yourself (aiming for financial independence) takes focus and sustained effort. Here are eight steps toward meeting your goals. Remember that, as with learning to walk, the trick is to take one step at a time.

1. **Start over if you need to.** If you've had a rough year or two – and who hasn't? – now is a great time to start rebuilding. Prioritizing your savings is a great place to start. So is repairing or re-establishing your credit. Start slow and remember not to bite off more than you can chew. Six months' worth of net income in the bank as an emergency fund is a good goal, as is making your payments on time, which will help raise your credit score.

2. **Share your goals.** Sharing financial goals with friends (or even on social media, with strangers) can help you articulate your top goals and hold yourself accountable. Whether it's money, health, or career, studies suggest that making public statements about plans helps people maintain a more substantial commitment to them.

3. **Work towards eliminating debt.** Don't be afraid to open your bank statements because you think you've spent too much money. Checking your statements regularly can ensure that

your checking accounts and credit cards are in line, and let you keep an eye out for proper return credits and false charges.

If you did spend more than you'd like, make a plan to pay off the debt. Figure out how much you can afford to pay each month. Post that amount somewhere you will see it every day, such as in your bedroom, bathroom, or closet. That constant reminder will help you make progress. Alternatively, you can use that calendar to keep track of your financial goals each month.

4. **Get your partner on the same financial page with you.** Coordinating your spending and savings habits with your partner can lead to a smoother relationship. It can also mean more money in your joint bank accounts. If you haven't already, sit down with your partner to discuss any goals or big plans they'd like to achieve financially. Even having a quick monthly get-together to review finances can be a productive and straightforward path to establishing healthy money habits in your relationship and avoiding fights about money in the future.

5. **Check your credit score and credit report.** You should be checking your credit report every 12 months at least. Doing so is free, an essential step in rebuilding and maintaining good credit, and integral to staying on top of your finances. The big three reporting agencies – Experian, TransUnion, and Equifax – provide

free annual credit reports, and some banks and credit cards offer a free copy of your score each month.

6. **Review your insurance policies.** Financial independence isn't all about saving and growing money: it's also important to protect what you have. Insurance can be a very effective means of protection. The types you may need include life, health, home, auto, and long-term care.

Contemplating our own death isn't much fun. But having a **life insurance** policy is essential to safeguarding your family's financial security. If you want to help ensure that no one will have to take care of you in your waning years, consider long-term care insurance, as well.

By the way, when I say that having insurance is wise, I'm not talking about paying a warranty on that new refrigerator that probably will not break down. I'm talking about insuring big-ticket items only such as your car, house, and health. Even then, push the deductible as high as you can. In the case of **car insurance**, make sure to insure against the other person with uninsured motorist protection. If I hadn't had ample amounts of this important coverage, my accident would have devastated me financially as well as physically. Reviewing your policies once a year is a great way to make sure they are in good standing, and you have enough coverage. You can also check if your employer offers supplemental coverage as part of your benefits. Make sure you've designated the correct beneficiaries!

7. **Revisit your budget.** Budgeting isn't a "write it and forget it" activity. It takes consistent review to keep it real. Are you spending more than your limits on groceries every month? Increasing your grocery budget may be the wisest course – while deciding what other expenditures to decrease so your monthly figures still balance out. Also, sometimes, changes happen. Maybe you want to take a trip and so are saving for that. Maybe you need a new furnace, or your house needs painting, or you want to buy a new car. Amending your budget to save for these things can ensure that you don't take on debt to pay for them.

8. **Remember to reward yourself.** Once you have your plan in place, make sure to reward yourself once you hit each milestone. Try not to make these rewards new purchases; instead, choose experiences that add to your mental and physical health such as a beautiful day of snowboarding or biking, or a game night with your loved ones. If you choose to splurge on a massage or day at the spa, make sure you can afford it. Budgeting in reward money is one way to treat yourself while staying on your course.

Remember, the best things in life are free. But it's much easier to enjoy those things if you have a robust financial system in place to help you weather any storm. That way, you'll be prepared for what is ahead, and you'll already be in the mindset for financial success.

Don't Just Dream It: Manifest It

"Manifesting" is a big word for visualizing your dreams and willing them into being. It's "making everything you want to feel and experience a reality... via your thoughts, actions, beliefs, and emotions," says Angelina Lombardo, the author of the book The Spiritual Entrepreneur. Learning and using manifesting methods can really help you to grow. Even if you've suffered hardships – as many of us did during the chaos of 2020 – you can move out of despair and into self-love using proven mental methods for making your dreams come true. Manifestation is one such method.

Compliment Sandwiches Are Delicious

Have you ever heard of a compliment sandwich? It is when you give praise, then constructive critiques, then conclude with praise and positivity.

This is how we should move out of our old ways of being and into the new – starting with recognition! Think about your accomplishments. What have you achieved this far in life?

Did you achieve a personal or financial goal?

Were you able to spend time with your family?

Or maybe you quit your job to pursue a passion.

Whatever has brought you joy in the past year, re-visit the experience, and re-experience the joy. Hold on to this feeling.

Now, offer yourself some constructive criticism. Could you have budgeted better, or created a more substantial work-life balance? If you were laid off, did you take on a victim mindset? How could you move out of that defeating stance more quickly?

Now, it's time for the other compliment to sandwich your self-critique. There's always more that we could do, and ways that we might have reacted better. Being human means being imperfect, and being imperfect means we have room for growth. Growth is not only good, but it's also exciting. When we stop growing – well, you know what that means.

Manifest and Prepare

Now that we have completed our compliment sandwich, it is time to look at the goals you set earlier in this chapter and begin manifesting them. Here are tips:

1. Start with a positive mindset. Cleanse your mind of negative or limiting thoughts or beliefs. Manifesting has worked for many success-

ful people including Oprah Winfrey, and it will for you, too.

2. Visualize – and feel – yourself accomplishing your goal. Picture it happening in as much detail as possible.

3. Ponder what you must do to achieve this goal and write down the steps.

4. Set mini achievements along your journey and celebrate even minor accomplishments.

5. Also, don't neglect the importance of self-care. Do you need a gym membership? Do you need a financial mentor? Make sure to clearly state what type of support you will need to manifest your desires!

There's nothing magical about manifestation – you're not conjuring something from nothing. As in all the steps and lessons in this book, achievement takes desire, dedication, action, and commitment.

Do these words sound familiar? They're what we're told we must have for a happy, healthy love relationship. And what better way to enact these principles than by creating and nurturing your love relationship with yourself.

Buh-Bye Budget:

How to Slim Down Your Body and Budget

Living your best life and implementing health and fitness into your daily routine will leave you feeling energized and prevent future health problems.

Gym memberships can be pricey, however. Whether you are on a budget or need to get inventive with your spending habits, read on to see all the creative ways you can stay fit without breaking the bank.

Set reasonable, realistic goals. Unless you have the money to pay for a personal trainer or have the time to exercise for multiple hours a day, remember to be gentle with yourself and celebrate the baby steps you take along your fitness journey. It can be as simple as making a choice to take the stairs instead of the elevator, bringing a home-cooked meal for your lunch, or parking on the far side of the parking lot while shopping. These small steps do add up and cost you absolutely nothing.

Decide the best way for you to work out and be creative. What is going to keep you on track and motivated? Is it finding a gym? Are you working out from home? Are you seeing a friend to keep you accountable?

If getting a gym membership doesn't fit in your budget right now, don't let that deter you from getting in a good workout. There are lots of free or inexpensive ways to get in shape if you think creatively:

- **Walking or running.** Walking or running just 30 minutes a day stimulates your brain to think about problems more creatively, keeps the pounds off, and can improve your mood. All you need is a good pair of shoes!

- **Biking.** Find a local trail or try cycling to work a few days a week.

- **Dog walking.** If you don't own a dog, borrow one from a family member or friend. Or find a shelter in need of volunteers to walk dogs. You can help your community and get your exercise.

- **Using free outdoor gyms.** Some city parks have open outdoor gyms where adults can work out. These "adult playgrounds" are usually made with simple but effective fitness equipment, such as rowing machines, leg presses, and stretching bars.

- **Special offers.** Many gyms offer trials memberships to new members, or you can find deals on discount sites like Groupon. If you're flexible, you could try a different gym each week or month.

- **Working out at home.** It's easy to create a simple, inexpensive space to get your sweat on. All you truly need for a home gym is

- room to move around, a computer/television to watch workout videos on, and a set of resistance bands or light weights.

For a complete gym, equipment such as an exercise ball, kettle-bells, jump rope, floor mat, and more can be helpful. Check out discount stores and online marketplaces like eBay and Craigslist for budget-friendly places to pick up used fitness equipment.

You can find an abundance of free workouts online or on sites such as YouTube, and phone apps offer free or cheap workout programs.

Can't find a workout that suits your fancy? You can achieve complete training with nothing more than your own body. Movements like squats, lunges, push-ups, burpees and jumping jacks offer a cheap and effective way to tone up.

Shop around for gym memberships. Gyms can be beautiful places to find motivation and inspiration to live your best life. Should you decide to join one, here are tips to matching the right one to your budget:

- **Choose local over chain.** The monthly fees at locally owned gyms are likely to be lower than at well-known chains, while offering the same necessary equipment.

- **Seek employer perks.** Ask your human resources department whether your company subsidizes workouts or offers any gym discounts for employees.

- **Shop for the best deal.** Many times, especially around the holidays, gyms will promote enticing special deals to boost sales. Do your research to see which gym is offering the cheapest rate.

- **Consider the punch card.** How many times a month do you go to the gym? If you rarely go, you might be spending thirty dollars or more per visit. Ask your gym if you can buy a class pack or a punch card to save you money.

There is no reason why getting healthy is too expensive to fit into any budget – it merely takes some extra planning and creativity.

Chapter 5

ADD IT UP

"Self-worth takes you further than net worth."
~Matshona Dhliwayo

How much are you worth? If you don't know the answer, join the club. Many people, I've found, don't know their net worth or how to find it. And if you don't know where you're starting in your money-fear-to-money-love journey, the goals map you drew in Chapter 4 won't take you far.

Just as you need to know where you want to go in your financial journey, it's important to understand where you stand financially today. Maybe your goal is to accumulate one million dollars. If you're starting with only a little cash and few investments, this goal could stress you out! But if your house is paid off or nearly so, you could be a lot closer to that million-dollar mark than you might have thought.

Financial independence means having enough money to take care of yourself without worries. How close are you now? You may be nearer – or farther away – than you think. Either way, if you want to be real about your financial life and goals, it's important to find out.

What Your Net Worth Is — and Isn't

First of all, let me reiterate: your net worth is not your self-worth. How much you have or what you own doesn't reflect the quality of your character; nor does it determine how lovable you are, no matter what your friends and family members tell you. (The Beatles were right: money can't buy you love.)

But your net worth – which equals your assets minus your debts – may play a part in determining where and how you live, when and how you'll retire, even how healthy you are. If you have a positive net worth and attainable goals, you're less likely to suffer anxiety, which is a key contributor to insomnia, high blood pressure, and other ailments. Not getting enough sleep also increases your risk of accidents and lowers your attention span, which can hurt your work performance. Money might not buy happiness, but a positive and growing net worth can give you much to smile about.

Net worth can include a lot of things:

- The money in your checking and savings accounts

- The money in your investment and retirement accounts

- The value of your house and car minus what you owe on them

- Your possessions that have value, such as art, antique furniture and dishes, or the coin collection you inherited from a long-lost uncle

- Insurance policies

- Royalties

- The business you own – whether or not you intend to sell it

Even your credit score counts – not as a checkmark on your financial statement, necessarily, but as a steppingstone to your financial independence. When did you last check yours?

As I mentioned in Chapter 4, any of the big three credit agencies will send your credit report to you for free once a year, and banks and credit-card companies often include credit-score reports with your monthly bill. Above and beyond the score, these reports can be a veritable treasure trove of information. They can apprise you of debts you might have forgotten, or to fraudulent activity that could drain your accounts or cause you a lot of hassle if your identity gets stolen.

What can make the report so frightening, though, isn't the overview of your financial activities, but that intimidating score. It's like getting a report card in school. The maximum score is 850. What if yours is lower? There's no shame: the number in no way reflects who you are. The average credit score in the U.S. is 698 – quite a bit short of perfection, and that average dips lower in some states.

My advice is: bite the bullet and find out your score. Then, when the good habits you're acquiring start to take effect, you'll get the satisfaction of watching the number rise.

Your credit report can tell you about the debts for which you've had bank loans: car loans, credit cards, student loans, and mortgages, for instance. But it doesn't show everything. You may have other kinds of debt and obligations taking your money away from where you want it to go.

To find where your money is going, examine your credit card bills and bank statements. Do you have subscriptions that you don't use, apps you've paid for, or streaming services? At $9.99 or more a month, these can really siphon off your income, draining your budget and hampering your ability to save.

And yet you may have forgotten that you even have some of these subscriptions. Perhaps you signed up to get them for free to watch a show or just to try the app, but when the trial period ended you never canceled, and are now paying for monthly or annual subscriptions. Now is the time to cancel. You can always resubscribe if you want to use the service again. And the next time you take advantage of a free trial, make a note on your calendar to cancel before the paid subscription period kicks in – or cancel right away, which only means that your card won't be charged later.

Banks have long used a similar method to entice people to switch to using their credit cards. They might offer zero interest for as long as one year, ostensibly giving you time and some leeway to pay off the balance. Of course, the bank won't make any money if you do that. Any leftover balances could suddenly, at the end of the zero-interest period, get smacked with a huge interest rate – as high as 36 percent. Make sure you read the fine print before signing up for these kinds of deals: as the saying goes, "If it sounds too good to be true, it probably is."

Adding up your assets – what you own – and subtracting your liabilities to find your net worth will give you the starting point from which to set your financial goals. But before you can start to build your asset kingdom, you need to get out of the red by tackling those pesky debts.

Fade that Red to Black

If your asset-to-debt ratio is in the negative range, it's time to really focus on whittling down your debt. Conventional wisdom says we should pay off debts with the highest interest rate first, but finance guru Dave Ramsey has a different approach: the "Debt Snowball Method."

In this debt-elimination round, you tackle your smallest debt first, paying as much as you can each month while paying the minimum on your other debts. As in making a snowball, you start small and grow as you go. Paying off smaller debts first gives you confidence and builds momentum, Ramsey says. The can-do feeling increases with each loan payoff so that you'll face your bigger debts with a sense of challenge instead of intimidation. You *can* do it!

Being free from debt is one of the most significant financial freedoms you can give yourself. It's also a form of self-respect. Debt can cause so much worry, anxiety, insecurity, and emotional pain. What would it feel like to you to be debt-free? Would you feel like a completely different person? The less debt you have, the more confidence and inner strength you will feel. You are worth that feeling of self-love and joy that being debt-free brings.

Dr. Karl Pillemer is a Cornell professor who has spent his career discussing the meaning of life with more than 1,200 senior citizens. The common theme he found among the members of this diverse group: worry. The vast majority said they spent too much time worrying.

Is this the life you want for yourself?

Life is precious. Life is short. Do you wish to spend yours with fear living rent-free in your head? You have the power to choose the kind of life you want to live – and this includes your financial life.

Turn that Worry Frown Upside Down

When a financial fear pops into your head, what do you feel? Chances are, it's anxiety. Calm yourself and take control by asking yourself three questions:

1. "What am I grateful for in this moment?" Our brains can't process anxiety and gratitude at the same time. Try focusing on the good things to send your anxieties running.

2. "What action or step can I take to alleviate this worry?" If worry has a positive function, it's to stimulate us to take action. Doing

something – even something small, like paying a bill, reviewing your investment accounts, or making a list of your expected income over the coming months – may increase your confidence.

3. "What can I learn from this moment that I want to remember?" Assigning a purpose to your worry session can renew your resolve for meeting your financial goals.

But the best answer of all is to not have money worries at all – and the best way to rid yourself of them is to eliminate your debt.

Seven Smart Steps to Debt-Free Living

Sixty-eight percent of U.S. adults with credit card debt told creditcards. com that they don't feel confident that they'll *ever* be able to pay theirs off. Thirty percent of people polled said they would never be debt-free, and another 38% said they're not sure if or when that day would come.

This doesn't have to be you. Follow these seven rules of thumb, and you can be on your way to true financial freedom.

Get real: Write out all the purchases adding to your debt so that you can account for each dollar spent. This may seem annoying and even stressful: think of it as a form of tough love.

Writing down each and every expenditure will help you to reduce them and your debts. People find themselves in debt due to many small purchases rather than a single big one. Taking pen in hand to put each of yours in writing will give you perspective on your spending and the reason for your debt.

Admit it. Be honest with yourself. Stop pretending that nothing is wrong. Ignoring your debt won't make it go away. Woman up! Man up! Person up! Admitting you have a problem is the first step to correcting it.

Add it up. To not let your debt define you, you must get honest with how significant your liability is. Pull out all those bills and every credit card and loan statement you own, and give them a long, hard look.

Be honest with yourself. This is going to hurt, but remember, tough love is still love. Figure out the current, correct balance of every debt you owe. Be sure to include how much you owe on your student loan, your car, your house, and – oh yes – your credit cards. How many of those do you have? Visualize your debt. Practice brutal honesty. Only when you know how much of a debt hole you are in can you begin climbing out of it.

Share it. I don't mean blasting your debt situation all over social media or telling a gossipy friend or family member. I'm talking about becoming accountable to yourself by sharing it with someone you trust.

You may feel shame; that's okay. Shame, like worry, can have an upside if it stimulates you to action. If your debt embarrasses you, you may feel more motivated to eliminate it. When you give voice to your problem by speaking it to another, it becomes real. No longer can you pretend that it doesn't exist. Now, you're accountable – not just to yourself, but to someone else.

Get smart. Once you're aware of your debts, make the effort to understand the liability terms. How much interest are you paying on each of these loans? How long will it take you to pay it off? An eye-opening exercise: adding up all the interest you're paying per year for the privilege of owning your debt. This figure alone will most likely motivate you to change your habits. It could be enough to buy you a nice vacation or even a car. Sticker shock yourself into action.

Make a plan. That giant sucking sound you hear is your money going down the drain. How long will you give yourself to stop it? Use one of the free financial calculators easily found online to set up a payment plan beyond the minimums. Making minimum payments only prolongs your debt – and enriches the bank.

For example: if your credit card has a $5,000 balance with an interest rate of 16% (which is on the low side these days), making a minimum payment of $100 a month would pay off your loan in about seven years. If you add $50 per month to that payment, you could pay it off in about four years.

Create a twenty-four-hour rule. Don't backslide into old habits by compromising your integrity and getting pulled into impulse purchases. Next time you "must have" that new black sweater (even if you already have three at home), hit the "pause" button. Tell yourself, "I'm not an impulse shopper. I like to think about purchases before I buy." Then, give yourself twenty-four hours to think about why you need this sweater. Maybe what you really need is resolve.

No one likes to watch the same horror show over and over again – or even, for some of us, once – especially when the horror show is our own life.

If paying off your debts seems an impossible dream and you start to feel discouraged, think about how much lighter you'll feel when you've paid it off. Growth is rarely comfortable, but remember, growing pains don't last. Suck it up, buttercup. Get real and start being true to yourself so you can have a financial future that will make you proud.

Eliminate the Negative, Accentuate the Positive

Becoming debt-free requires patience and discipline. Having goals for what you'll do with your money after those credit card balances are gone can be a source of motivation and inspiration. But again, it's important to keep it real.

Some goals are critical for the short term, but others will require patience and fortitude. In the same way in which you whittled away at your debts until they disappeared, you'll add incrementally to your investments for the future.

But you can't do everything at once. Progress requires baby steps and focus on one goal at a time. I suggest making three lists of asset-building goals, starting with the now, progressing to the near future, and moving ahead to the farther horizon.

Short term: First, build your emergency fund, a cash reserve fund containing three to six months of your living expenses kept in an easily accessible account such as a savings account at your bank or credit union. When an urgent need arises – a medical emergency or a home repair – you'll have the money on hand to pay for it instead of needing to go into debt. Avoiding debt where possible is the name of the game. Then, you'll replenish this fund as quickly as you can before resuming your kingdom-building campaign.

Medium term: Once your emergency fund is in place, you can start saving for medium-term goals: a vacation, perhaps, or a new (to you) car. (New cars are almost never a good idea, since they lose value the moment you drive them off the lot. I recommend shopping around for a good used vehicle instead.)

Long term: What are your goals for ten years from now? Twenty? Perhaps you'd like to retire, take a trip around the world, or pay for your children's or grandchildren's college education. The farther ahead you can plan for these goals, the better. The money you'll invest to fund them will increase on their own over time, meaning that you may need to use less of your money now to reach your desired goal. You'd be surprised how much twenty dollars a week can grow over twenty years!

What Will Your Golden Years Look Like?

Will your retirement dreams match your reality? That's perhaps the most critical question to ask people who are currently retired. Is your retirement what you expected, or is it something else?

For most, retirement is the "next chapter" in life. Your finances must support your retirement vision, so there are no surprises when it's your turn. But the exigencies of everyday living often cause people to neglect their retirement accounts. Often, they promise themselves that they'll start investing tomorrow – but that "tomorrow" never comes.

If this is you, beware. Before you know it, you're like one of my clients who came to me in her late 50s with only $38,000 in her retirement fund. I helped her to see – with some tough love – how she was hurting herself. Did she want to work all the way to the grave? And – what if she wasn't physically or mentally able to do so? Thirty-eight thousand wouldn't last more than a year, if that.

This client is self-employed and has no employer matching her retirement contributions. That made her situation even tougher. But I helped her set up a Self-Employment Plan, or SEP – a retirement plan that's tax-deferred, meaning she'll only pay taxes on the money as she withdraws it, and a Roth IRA, with contributions taxed now but not when the money comes out. She also eventually opened a non-retirement investment account in which her money buys stocks and bonds. At 60, she's now on track to reach $1 million in investments by the time she's 70 – if she doesn't retire before then. What's more, she refinanced her mortgage to a 15-year loan with a low interest rate and makes extra payments on the principal each month. She's on track to pay off her house by the time she's 68.

It's Never Too Late

As a financial advisor, I've seen that it is never too late to change your retirement path. Are you planning to rely on Social Security? I hope not. It's designed as a supplement, not to cover even your baseline living expenses. If you hope to ever retire, you must proactively save to supplement your Social Security checks.

The best retirement plan relies on income from three pillars, like the three legs of a stool: Social Security, qualified plans such as IRAs, 401Ks, company pension plans, and SEPs, and investments other than retirement. This three-legged model provides you with a firmer platform from which to handle any changes that might come your way – for, as we know, the change is the only constant in life.

The more money you have set aside, the more options you will have. Don't count on a stable economy: as we've seen with recent events, things beyond our control can send inflation soaring and cause the stock market to drop. Don't count on dying by a certain age: life expectancy continues to rise, and I've too often seen people underestimate how long they'll live.

If your retirement funds are low, you can increase them. One way is by dollar-cost averaging.

What is dollar-cost averaging, and how does it work?

- In the financial world, dollar-cost averaging refers to systematically saving a specific amount into an investment.

- An example would be to transfer $100 a month from your checking account into an investment such as a mutual fund at the same time every month.

- If you can systematically invest in an investment that fluctuates in value, you buy your asset when your money is received.

The easiest and most effective way to grow your retirement savings is to hire a financial advisor who can help you build a diversified portfolio.

If you want to stay on the safe side, you might place your money in certificates of deposit or money market funds – but be aware that these will provide a lower rate of return. Some are investing in cryptocurrencies. If you're curious about them, do understand that their value fluctuates wildly. Also, crypto isn't regulated or governed in any way, at least not at the time of writing this book.

Stocks and bonds also fluctuate in value, but they tend to be less volatile than crypto. Their prices are based on supply and demand and will bounce around throughout the day while the exchange matches the orders to sell and buy.

By systematically accumulating shares each month with your investment, you will collect more when the market dips, like buying something "on sale." If you buy something at $10 a share and the price drops to $5, your next deposit could buy you two shares – something you'll appreciate when the price goes up again.

Price fluctuation is what makes dollar-cost averaging so effective over time. Think of it as buying something you will need for the future. And if you can buy it at a discount, even better. Instead of panicking when your stocks decrease in value, you can rub your hands together in glee, knowing that you'll get more for your money with this month's investment!

It's human nature to want to let your investments ride in a "bull market," when prices are rising. For long term investments, it's best to stay the course in a "bear market," when prices are low, as well. If you've cashed out when prices dip, it won't be as easy to rebound when they rise again. Dollar-cost averaging is an excellent solution to determine when to enter or exit the market.

Here's how to start dollar-cost averaging:

1. Participate in your employer's retirement plan. Your employer will deduct funds from your paycheck and send them to your retirement account. They may send a matching amount which

will help you accumulate funds faster. Doing this is the best way to give yourself a raise!

2. Set up a Roth IRA if you qualify, and transfer funds into it monthly.

3. Set up an investment program through your financial advisor or a mutual fund company. It's easy and efficient and, chances are, you won't even miss those funds.

4. Buy stock in a favorite company that pays dividends, and sign up for a dividend reinvestment plan, or DRIP, which allows you to, instead of taking your dividends in cash, reinvest them by buying more shares of the stock.

Technology has made it easier to invest with small amounts, but to benefit from dollar-cost averaging, you must take action.

Inflation is the most significant threat you face in retirement. Having different types of savings and creating various income sources can help you stay fiscally nimble so you can enjoy your retirement without stressing over where the money you need to live will come from.

Make Your Life Count — Literally

Counting up your assets and liabilities can be intimidating, especially if your income is low and/or your debts high. But to set goals, you need a starting point. From here, you can look ahead to brighter days when you've got the money to pay cash for the things you want, interest free, or you can retire early and write that book you've always wanted to write, or take a trip around the world, or something else. Your desires will manifest by your intentions, planning, and self-discipline.

You deserve to live your best life. You can have the life you have always dreamed of. To get there, you'll need to stay determined and be unflinchingly honest with yourself. Working toward financial independence is the very best gift you can give to yourself – and you are worth it!

Chapter 6

READY, SET, GO!

"Dreams don't work unless you take action.
The surest way to make your dreams come true is to live them."
~Roy T. Bennett

Rubber, meet road.

In this chapter, you get to put into action the philosophies and tenets you've learned so far. Your goals set, your mindset shifted, and your map to financial independence drawn, you're ready to start living the good life – one in which you use your money *not* as a form of self-sabotage, but as a tool for self-love.

Living the Lifestyle of the Rich and Famous...

...is not what you think. Sure, we read about uber-wealthy men with expensive hobbies like Tesla Motors founder Elon Musk's SpaceX and the million-dollar yachts of Russian oligarchs. But most of the wealthy people I've known have been more like Berkshire Hathaway CEO Warren Buffet, the "Oracle of Omaha."

Buffet is widely known as a frugal billionaire. Most days, he eats breakfast at McDonald's. Once, in Singapore, he took Microsoft founder Bill Gates, who says Buffet pulled out coupons to reduce the price of their order even more. He buys his cars at a discount and drives them until his daughter says, "Um, Dad, it's starting to get embarrassing."

Buffet lives in the house he bought in 1957, in Omaha, Nebraska. With a $100 billion net worth, he could afford a luxury penthouse or mansion anywhere in the world. And he's a bargain hunter, he reportedly told interviewer Piers Morgan in 2013, "Whether we're talking about socks or stocks, I like buying quality merchandise when it is marked down."

Why would one of the world's richest people live this way? Well – how do you think Buffet got to be so wealthy? It sure wasn't from living above his means.

One thing that makes his story so delightful is that Buffet seems to derive a gleeful enjoyment from saving money. Imagine a multi-billionaire presenting Egg McMuffin buy-one-get-one-free coupons at McDonald's with his multi-billionaire friend looking on. Does the man have no shame? Not when it comes to taking care with his money, it seems. But there's no shame at all in loving yourself.

For Buffet, buying those socks on sale is every bit as much a game as buying stocks when the market dips. The same applies to most wealthy people I've known. They get a charge out of comparison shopping, clipping coupons, estate sales, and rummaging through the bargain bin. They aren't depriving themselves: they're having fun! They're treating themselves by saving as much as they can on purchases, so they have more to invest in themselves.

For example, I hardly ever dine out in restaurants in the town where I live. It's not that there aren't good ones – there are. But I have a nice kitchen at home and enjoy cooking meals with my husband. I'd rather save the money, and the calories, for my next vacation. When I travel, I'm all about fancy hotels and great restaurants.

Someone else might travel on a budget but wear designer fashions. Another might shop in vintage clothing stores but drive a fancy car.

The point of financial independence isn't to deprive yourself of anything, but to prioritize according to your income, goals, and values. Like Buffet, you can make a game of it, finding joy in being thoughtful with your money instead of spending impulsively. You can find bliss in the self-love of pursuing financial security rather than self-sabotage by overspending on things you don't cherish or need.

Does that mean you won't have to make sacrifices? Not at all. In fact, you probably will have to forgo something you want – very much, perhaps – from time to time. But instead of thinking about what you aren't getting, try shifting your focus to what you will receive.

I visited an art gallery with a friend who is comfortably retired, and she saw a painting that she absolutely loved. It was reasonably priced, too. The gallery owner, seeing her eyeing the piece, offered her a discount – but my friend declined. "That's the price of a plane ticket," she said. As much as she likes art, she likes traveling more.

I've never met a self-made person who isn't price conscious. Those with inheritances or trust funds may spend more freely, but financially independent people who've worked for their wealth do not tend to buy impulsively. They carefully consider not only *what* they should purchase, but *why* and *whether*, as well as *when*. They spend their money on items that bring them joy and that they genuinely value – not on a piece of clothing or jewelry to wear once and put away.

Fearless Does *Not* Mean Reckless

What's the definition of "courage"? Merriam Webster calls it "mental or moral strength to venture, persevere, and withstand danger, fear, or difficulty."

Notice that the word "reckless" doesn't appear in this definition. Recklessness means "marked by lack of proper caution: careless of consequences." The second definition is, "irresponsible."

Which does it mean – reckless or courageous – to spend more than we make, taking on debt, thinking only of today and hardly at all of tomorrow? "Devil may care," throwing caution to the wind, YOLO: (you only live once) our culture enshrines these attitudes and approaches. To me, casting a blind eye to the consequences of our behaviors seems not courageous, but cowardly.

A woman I know – let's call her Pam – provides a great example of how it's possible to spend cautiously yet live the "good life" at the same time. Pam is a successful realtor who lives in a nice, but modest home. She's always elegantly dressed in classic styles – that she buys at thrift stores and secondhand boutiques. She rides public transportation except when she's showing properties. For these occasions, she drives a very nice, impeccably appointed car.

Outgoing Pam also has an active social life that costs her virtually nothing. The consummate networker, she attends business social functions in part for the free food. She's the unofficial queen of her city's happy hour, and she knows all the best values for food and drink. When she wants to attend a pricier event such as a symphony, concert, or a weekend food festival, she volunteers. And yet, Pam does splurge on the things that matter to her, taking her children and grandchildren on trips and participating in family outings.

Pam understands that being careful with her spending isn't the same as depriving herself. She enjoys life as much as anyone I know, while spending less money even than most people who stay home every night.

True courage doesn't involve casting your fears to the wind or pretending they don't exist. It involves looking them in the eye with compassion until they transform into something else – such as love.

Mind Your Money-Dos

Old habits die hard. It's easy to slip back into them, even when we know they aren't serving us. But it's easier to repair the track before the train arrives than to put the train back onto the tracks after it has derailed. To help you stay on your path to financial freedom, here are some money-dos to practice day by day.

Money-Do: Keep Journaling

At the start of this book, you began a money journal. I hope you're still keeping it. Neuroscience has shown that writing down your thoughts helps shape your behaviors – and the physical act of putting pen or pencil to paper reinforces your changes even more.

Try to write in your money journal every day, perhaps listing three goals and three things you are grateful for. Be sure leaf through your notebook from time to time to remind yourself of what you're trying to achieve as well as challenges you've faced, and to see how far you've come.

Money-Do: Break It Down

Dreaming big is important but doing big can feel overwhelming. That's why, when making sweeping plans, it's best to break the actions needed to fulfill them into smaller, discrete parts.

Ready, set, go: To accomplish any task, big or small, break it into smaller pieces, then start with the first step. That way, you'll create a linear trail of dots that begin right now, at this moment, and end with your goal. Building your emergency fund, the next "money-do," provides a great example of this approach in action.

Money-Do: Build Your Emergency Fund

Have you figured out yet that saving money is pretty much the key to everything? And the first money you save should go into your emergency fund, also known as "saving for a rainy day."

An emergency fund is to your financial life what a net is to a high-wire acrobat. The goal is to *not* fall, but if you do, your emergency fund can protect you from disaster.

Ready: How much should you save? Conventional wisdom advises three to six months' expenses.

Make a list of your must-pay monthly bills, leaving off the "nice to have" items in your budget: this is your base amount. Add up these expenses and multiply by three to get the minimum amount you will need.

Set reasonable goals for building your fund. Start with an amount that seems doable, say $1,000, and a timeframe that you feel comfortable meeting, say, one year. To save $1,000 in one year, you need only contribute $83.33 per month. Can you find room in your budget for this expense – by eating one less meal out per month, perhaps, or taking public transportation instead of driving to work?

If you're still struggling to save, try setting up automatic deposits of cash from your checking account into savings. In this way, you pay yourself first, then pay for everything else with the remaining income. Chances are very good that, in time, you'll forget to miss the money coming off the top of your paycheck, and you'll have a very pleasant surprise waiting when the year is up – peace of mind.

Go: For what may you use the money from your emergency fund? For emergencies only! Make a pact with yourself listing the types of events that you're allowed to fund from this account. Hint: weddings and vacations should not be included on this list.

Events for which you might use this fund include losing your job, experiencing a medical emergency, having a car breakdown, needing an urgent home repair, or needing to travel for an emergency reason such as a funeral. Resist the temptation to dip into this fund for any other reason. If you want something but can't afford it, say no. Saying no to spending now is the same as saying yes to security and peace of mind for the rest of your life.

Money-Do: Weed Out What's Not Working

After you've had a budget in place for several months, it's time to reassess. Are you consistently overspending in some areas? If so, perhaps you need to increase your allotted amount for those categories. Or maybe you'll decide, instead, to reassess your spending in this area.

Ready, set, go: It's a good idea to take stock of all you're doing in life and discern what you should keep and what to toss.

Do you really need $50 bottles of wine? Many truly delicious wines sell for much less. Scout out a wine shop, get to know the person in charge, and ask them for recommendations. As they get to know you better, they should be able to direct you to bargain bottles you will enjoy, which can save you a bundle over time. Also, pay attention to your alcohol consumption. Recent studies show that having even one drink a night can cause damage to your brain, and it can be bad for your budget, as well. Consider making delicious mocktails from soda and tonic water, fruit juices, and other yummy ingredients.

Do you really need to drive your car to the office and pay for parking? A bus pass can be so much more affordable, lets you avoid traffic jams, and gives you time to clear your mind in preparation for the day ahead, or to wind down at day's end.

Do you really need to dine in expensive restaurants? Why not follow the example of my friend Pam and use Groupons in places you haven't tried before. Or scout out the low-cost happy hours in your town. Or invite friends to your place, and prepare meals from fresh ingredients that will be healthier and less expensive than food in restaurants, where chefs routinely boost flavors with unnecessary salt, fat, and sugar.

For more tips on cutting back on food costs, check out the sidebar to this chapter, **"Buh-Bye, Budget: Tips for Eating Healthy on a Bare-Bones Budget."**

Money-Do: Feed Your Financial Brain

If you're intimidated by money or the topic bores you, step out of your discomfort zone by educating yourself. Yes, having smart and conscientious financial planners managing your investments is crucial for reaching financial independence, but it's important to understand what they are doing, why, and how – after all, it's *your* money.

Ready, set, go: Boning up on money matters can be fun. Do you like podcasts? There are many good ones to listen to during your commute, your daily run, or while preparing meals. Suze Orman, a popular financial columnist whose advice specifically targets women, has a twice-weekly podcast called "Money and Women." Dave Ramsey, whose advice on paying off debt we've already explored in this book, has a podcast, too.

If you're not into podcasts, education and advice come in many others forms: books, blog posts, videos, TV shows, even classes you can attend in person or online – whichever suits your learning style.

Money-Do: Invest Wisely and With Wisdom

Your love affair with yourself is no fling, but a long-term commitment. That's why it's important to keep your eye on the big picture, not only when making decisions about your day-to-day and month-to-month spending, but also regarding your investments.

Investing your money is how you make it grow. Stocks, bonds, mutual funds, commodities, and other equities grow in value over time in a way that money sitting in your checking or savings account does not. But all these types of investments will fluctuate in value: some days their value will increase; on other days, they'll decline.

Over time, though, these types of investments do earn money. The stock market's average return over the last thirty years amounts to roughly ten percent – slightly less if you factor in inflation. Still, that's a vastly higher rate of return on your investments than even the most generous checking or savings account will provide – and it's a year-over-year number, compounded.

If you invest $10,000 today and add nothing, in ten years your money is likely to have earned $15,000 more. Just think what you could accumulate with monthly payments to the pot using dollar-cost averaging as we explained in Chapter 5!

This is what people mean when they say, "Your money should work for you, not the other way around."

Ready, set, grow: To succeed for us, our investments need time and space. Yes, I know, when the stock market falls, you may feel that sinking feeling in the pit of your stomach as well. But take heart: your ship won't go down, especially if you have a quality financial advisor by your side. What goes down *will* come up. You need only ride the wave with a steady keel and keep your gaze on the horizon. The trick is not to panic and jump ship.

Selling in a fluster because prices are dropping is how investors lose money that they can never get back. When you do this, it's very difficult to recoup your losses, even if you buy again later. The seasoned investor will view a dip in the as an opportunity to buy more stock with less money, which means more value when markets rise again (as they invariably do). "Sell high; buy low" is an oft-repeated mantra for good reason.

That's not to say that investing your money isn't a risk. It is. But it's a pretty safe one if you're willing to ride the wave through the downs as well as the ups. Panicking in a downturn and selling is almost always a bad idea, because we don't tend to make good decisions based on fear.

Of course, nothing can trigger our darkest unconscious fears – of homelessness, poverty, death – like money. If dealing with your finances causes you discomfort? Good! Think of your discomfort as growing pains. No pain, no gain.

Money-Do: Adopt a Spending Mantra

Remember my friend Pam, who decided against buying a painting she liked by reminding herself that the price equaled a plane ticket? Having a phrase of your own to help you weigh the importance of a tempting purchase now against a future goal can really help you to make your dreams come true.

Ready, set, go: Ask yourself: what can I say the next time I'm tempted that will help me get to no? Examples include: "Sale is a four-letter word." "For example, ask yourself, "Will I enjoy this purchase more than a trip to Bali next year?" or "I only charge items that cost $30 or more."

Money-Do: Believe in Yourself

If you're reading this book, chances are good that you've let your fears keep you from accomplishing what you've wanted to achieve in the financial realm. Maybe you're struggling with debt, or with saving for retirement, or don't know how you'll pay for college for your children. You need help – and you're counting on me to give you the answers you need.

With decades of financial planning and advising under my belt – not to mention starting my own the financial management company – I do have many suggestions and ideas for how anyone can turn around money's role in their lives from an object of fear to an instrument of love. But I can only lead you to the fountain. I can't drink the water for you.

To live your best life – whatever that means to you – you must not let your doubts and fears gain the upper hand, or if they do, you must step up and take it back for yourself.

You may experience doubts. "I'm so late to the game," you may think. "I can never catch up." But it's never too late! You may fear that you are too old, or not smart enough, or have too many obstacles in your way to realizing your dreams. But I'm here to tell you that you *can* do it! Truly, you need only to believe in yourself, and to put those beliefs into action.

Ready, set, go: Pick a dream or goal that you feel passionate about attaining: buying your dream home, starting your own business, taking that once-in-a-lifetime vacation, sending your children or grandchildren to college, etc. Visualize yourself fulfilling the desire. Create something like a collage or poem or painting or piece of music that can help to inspire you when you feel disheartened or discouraged. You've got this. Now is *your* time!

Money-Do: Strive for Balance

I'm not a fan of extreme situations. I don't want to see my clients depriving themselves of pleasures and joy today for the sake of tomorrow. Not to be maudlin, but what if tomorrow never comes?

Living joyously now while preparing for later requires a delicate balancing act. We must balance short-term with long-term, highs with lows, work with pleasure, frugality with splurging, generosity with self-care, and so much more.

You can find your balance. In doing so, you can have it all: the bedazzlement of now *and* the anticipation for the tomorrow you want to create for yourself.

If you live with the right balance, you can focus your energy and attention on things that matter. As you do, you may find yourself buying less. You may be surprised by how rewarding it can be to live on fewer resources. You may enjoy your possessions more.

You can live fully in the moment and also feel confident that tomorrow is taken care of – because *you* are taking care of it. You can let go of worries and focus your energies, instead, on enjoying life and all the magic it brings.

Buh-Bye Budget: Travel Hacks to Vacay Like a Pro

We can always travel in our dreams. Do you imagine yourself on a sunny beach, or hiking in a splendid alpine meadow with mountain views, or enjoying the many charms of your favorite European city?

Alas, the one thing that hasn't changed about travel is its cost. Of course, reading the luxury magazines may cause you to believe that only wealthy people can afford to go anywhere. But I'm here to tell you that budget traveling is not only possible, but it's highly enjoyable.

I know a man who travels the world on his bicycle and hardly spends a penny doing it. He works at his job in Australia for a year or two, saving every penny that he can until he amasses $10,000, and then he takes off on another journey. He can travel for a year at a time this way or even longer by staying with people for free via the Couchsurfing app and doing favors for them instead of paying money. He cooks his own meals – oatmeal and bananas every morning, vegetable stir-fries, and other inexpensive but nutritious foods. This man lives one of the most interesting lives of anyone I have ever met.

Despite what luxury magazines and travel agents tell you, it is entirely possible – and easy – to go on the vacation of your dreams without spending a small fortune. And, no, you don't have to ride a bicycle.

All you need is desire, research, and planning. It can be more work to travel thriftily, but it beats daydreaming about trips you never take.

Here are some of my best tips for saving money on travel while still having a blast:

Choose a Destination that Fits Your Budget.

- Say yes to unexpected opportunities.

- Check out locations where the American dollar can stretch farther, such as Thailand, Nepal, India, and Latin America.

- Don't stop at looking for cheap flights. Take care to consider how much the entire trip will cost, including lodging, food, and excursions.

- Consider unexpected destinations to fly into, such as Iceland, Finland, or Paris, and research the year's best times to travel to your destination. From these airports you may be able to fly or take the train cheaply to other destinations.

- If you have your heart set on a more expensive locale, try booking off-season, where you'll see fewer crowds and get better deals on hotels.

- Be flexible. Flights can be less expensive if you leave and return on certain days of the week. Hotels, too, can offer lower rates on certain days of the week.

Try to Plan Ahead of Time

- Bundling your bookings in advance by using websites like Expedia and Kayak can help you save more than if you book your hotel, airfare, and excursions separately.

- Think "Travel Tuesday:" Tuesdays are usually the cheapest day of the week to travel as well as to book your tickets, due to the low demand for flights on this day.

- Research public transportation options at your destination such as buses, trains, and light rail to avoid expensive taxis.

- Get comfortable with being uncomfortable. The cheapest travel options might not be the most convenient or practical. However, don't forget to treat yourself occasionally. A slight nod to luxury is often the battery charge you need to refuel you for the next stage of your journey.

Stretch Your Dollar Like a Pro

- Do as the locals do. Pro travel tip: excursions, bars, restaurants, and hotspots listed by travel guides – even those listed as "off the beaten path" – usually aren't a secret. Anything a business promotes to tourists is likely to be marked up. Instead, pay attention to where the locals go. Look for menus without English or ask your hotel concierge or bartender where the best neighborhood spots are.

- Collect experiences, not things. With souvenirs becoming less local and more mass-produced, focus on the memories you could have (a show, train ride, museum, et cetera) instead buying trinkets to bring home.

- Learn to haggle. Although in America, haggling isn't widely practiced as in many countries, you may be able to get a better deal just by asking.

- Bring your snacks when you are out and about. It will prevent you from spending money at tourist-trap restaurants, so you can save your cash for more authentic food.

Traveling on a dime requires research and determination, but with any luck you'll will come home with stories that money literally can't buy.

So How Do I Save Up Enough to Get Away?

Having a trip all paid up before you go dramatically reduces your chances of having to suffer and struggle when you return. For me, this means planning and saving for three to six months before embarking on that journey. How long it takes you to marshal your resources depends on your circumstances and on the kind of trip you plan.

Here are my recommendations:

- **Estimate your costs.** How much will airfare and other transportation, lodging, food and drink, and other expenses cost? Do you already have the money you need to pay these costs without raiding your emergency fund?

- If the answer is "no," you need a plan. Divide your estimate by the number of months until you leave, then automatically save that amount into a separate vacation account. The key here is *action*: if you don't put this money into its fund, you may spend it impulsively on other purchases.

- **Cut down on costs by thinking creatively.** Some credit cards offer rewards that you can redeem for travel or lodging. AAA discounts and Internet specials can also reduce expenses—especially if your travel dates are flexible. You might be surprised by how much you can shave off the cost of your trip!

- **Shift expectations to meet your reality.** Do not raid your long-term money for a short-term need. If you don't have the cushion in your budget to pay for a vacation at a Mexican beach or celebrity spa, consider visiting a national park instead. You'll get outside, find time for reflection (and maybe even get some exercise), and come home with a mind free of money worries. Then you can start planning for next year's luxury beach getaway.

Buh-Bye Budget: Tips for Eating Healthy on a Bare-Bones Budget

Benjamin Franklin said, "Failing to plan is planning to fail." Each of us has many priorities in our everyday lives; sometimes, as much as we would like to eat healthily, the hectic nature of our daily lives gets in the way of our doing so.

Fast foods are tempting to eat when your budget is about to go into the red; however, the key to eating healthy is to follow Mr. Franklin's advice and plan.

Why am I talking about health in a money book? If you live in the United States and have paid the costs of medical care, you should have little trouble connecting the dots. Nutrition plays a vital role in health, but giant plastic bottles of soda pop and bags of chips come very cheaply and can be tempting to someone with little time or money to spend.

Healthy meal prepping, grocery shopping, and maintaining a tight budget can be tricky, but it's doable. Read on to learn how to make sticking to your budget *and* eating healthy a piece of cake.

Plan Your Meals in Advance

The Internet is a treasure trove of free ideas and recipes for healthy meals. You might even find yourself branching out into new cuisines.

If you don't own a slow cooker, invest in one. These are so convenient, enabling you to cook meals in advance for the week or to start a meal before leaving for work.

Consider joining the loyalty or rewards program at the grocery store or stores where you shop, for discounts on your purchases. You can also check out your grocery store's weekly flyer in the newspaper or promotional emails or download coupons via the various coupon apps available. Using coupons helps you plan your meals around what's cheapest that week.

Know Before You Go

Write down what you will eat each day for breakfast, lunch, and dinner, as well as drinks and snacks.

Once you have an idea of what your weekly menu will look like and make your grocery list. Decide what you need to buy and what you already have or can use as a substitute.

While shopping, learn how to read price labels: look at the label for "price per ounce" (usually the number on the left side of the price tag). Analyzing this number will ensure you are getting the most of your money instead of being fooled by package sizes.

Prepare, Prepare, Prepare

The price of fresh produce can quickly double or triple your grocery budget. Here are some tips to keep it within your budget:

- **Buy fresh.** Remember that whole, unprocessed foods are more nutritionally dense and cheaper than processed foods. Yes, a bag of chips may be less expensive, but health-wise, produce is going to save you money in the long run.

- **Buy in season.** Buy fruits and veggies when they are in season, slice or prepare them, and freeze them. You can eat fresh all year round, even when produce isn't in season.

- **Make stock.** Try making vegetable or chicken stock for soups and other dishes.

- **Pack your lunch.** Prepare your lunches and snacks in advance so you have them ready when you're hungry, avoiding spending on lunches out or unhealthy snacks.

- **Grow your own herbs and vegetables.** If your apartment is small, consider container planting on your balcony or in sunny windows.

- **Get creative with leftovers.** If you cook a chicken over the weekend, you can extend it into your meals in different ways all week. Spending the energy to cook something once instead of throughout the week is intelligent and wallet friendly.

Shop With a Purpose.

The bulk section is your friend! Save money by stocking up on pasta, rice, oats, herbs, and spices when they go on sale.

Try ordering online, then picking up your groceries curbside. This method allows you to add items to your cart from home while checking your cupboards for what you have. It saves you time and money because you won't be making impulse purchases while walking the aisles in-store.

Chapter 7

LOVE AND MONEY

"Use money and love people. Don't love money and use people."
~Joseph Prince

"Money can't buy me love," the Beatles song goes, and boy, did they get that right. Having money doesn't necessarily make couples happier; sometimes, it's quite the opposite. One partner inheriting a large sum can cause problems in the relationship, for example. Study after study shows that financial problems are one of the top reasons why couples fight and even divorce.

Of course, money itself isn't causing the trouble. As we've seen, money is an inert object, unable to do anything on its own. Often, it's a symbol that stands for something else, even for love itself. Money can hold so many projections and be so fraught with emotions, including fear, that people in general have a difficult time talking about it. It's not money itself that's the issue, but people's inability to communicate about money.

Love and money go together about as well as oil and vinegar, in many cases. And it's not just romantic love that can suffer; financial issues can take their toll on parent-child and other family relationships, as well as friendships. Consider these common scenarios:

- An adult repeatedly asks their parent for money

- A friend expects another, more successful friend to pick up the tab when they go out

- One partner in a couple comes home with a – surprise! – expensive new car or concert tickets or new dress that isn't in the budget

I've known people in these situations and others like them, and I'll bet you have, too. Why can't love and money just get along?

Here's a hint: you know how it's said that, before you can love someone else, you first have to love yourself? I think the same holds true with money. To successfully navigate and defuse the money landmines in relationships, we first need to be able to set, communicate, and enforce boundaries, which is a form of self-respect born of self-love. And when we see money as a tool best used to love ourselves and others, we can treat it accordingly.

Giving our grown children endless amounts of money isn't love; it's enabling whatever lifestyle they're living that isn't supporting them.

Letting our friends take advantage of us isn't loving them or ourselves.

Letting our partner or spouse get away with spending our joint money on impulsive, extravagant items that we haven't discussed isn't love, but instead creates a breeding ground for resentment that will only hurt us both later and could potentially destroy our relationship.

It Takes Two to Tango — and to Talk About Money

Not being able to talk about finances – to ask for a raise at work; to tell our friends, "It's not in my budget" when they want us to do something with them; to collaborate on a budget and money goals with our romantic partner or spouse; to tell a family member, "I'm sorry, I can't help you" when we need to – only sets us up for fiscal failure and risks creating problems in our relationships.

Have you ever loaned money to a friend? You may feel generous in the moment, but over time you may wish you'd offered to co-sign with them on a loan application at their bank. Lending money to friends or family members can be risky business. What if they don't repay you? How would that affect your relationship? There's a reason why Shakespeare wrote, "Never a borrower nor a lender be." Even if everything works out as agreed, the transaction could change the nature of your relationship: if they can't pay you back as promised, they may feel guilty and avoid you; you may judge them.

With a spouse, the stakes rise even higher. Getting married means combining your resources to build your kingdom together, right? But if your values are different – maybe he likes to gamble, while you are a saver – those values might clash unless you're both able to "talk the talk."

Of course, after the wedding isn't the best time to discover that your approaches to money don't mesh. If you haven't yet tied the knot or moved in together, now is the time to ask yourself and your partner some very important questions.

Look Before You Leap

When you are wildly in love with someone, the very idea of moving in together can feel like heaven. Cohabitating lets you "try before you buy," letting you experience all the quirks you can only see in someone when you live with them before, or instead of, committing yourself to marriage. Or maybe you're skipping the moving-in-together phase and heading directly to the altar.

But don't move so fast. Stop and ask yourself if you and your beloved are ready for this step. Do you have the information you need to know that you're compatible, including your respective values and approaches to money?

If you're independent and they need to be in control, you could be headed for trouble. If you want separate bank accounts but they insist on joint, ditto. If they're freewheeling with money, extravagant spenders with a lot of credit card debt, but you're a careful, to-the-penny budgeter who'd rather save for a rainy day, it's best to know this before you join households and hearts.

Breaking a lease is a lot easier than divorcing, but it can be just as painful, and could leave you emotionally and financially drained.

Guard your heart by pondering these questions and their answers before you decide whether to make this truly big move:

1. Why do you want to live together? Do you want to move in with this person, or do you feel like you have to? Are they pressuring you? Or do you feel pushed into the move by some other external factor, such as losing your job or having your rent go up?

2. Does your lifestyle line up with your potential partner's? If you want children and they don't, the relationship could go south quickly. If you like to go out on the town but they'd rather stay home – and they want you at home with them most nights, or you want them out with you – one of you might end up disappointed. If you love to entertain but they don't like having people over, life could end up being no fun for one of you. If one of you is a stickler for cleanliness and the other is more relaxed about household chores, conflicts could very well ensue. And so on.

3. What are your expectations for daily chores?

4. If you have pets and your potential partner doesn't, will they be able to accept your pets? Will they help with veterinary bills?

5. What are your financial expectations? Who will be in charge of paying your joint bills? Some couples assign this task to one per-

son; others switch back and forth; others divide the bills among both partners.

6. Will you have a joint account for shared bills?

7. Will you divide the amount each of you pays on bills equally, or according to income?

8. Would you want to have a joint credit card? What would be the parameters for using it?

9. How do each of your life goals and dreams align? This is a great topic for your initial "dream date" nights, in which you talk about mutual wants and needs and how to pay for them.

10. Do you have a backup plan? If for any reason you find yourself "suddenly single," you'll rely on your nest egg or other financial safety net to keep you from crashing down.

After you've answered these questions – and written in your journal (don't forget to record your thoughts and feelings) you can then decide whether cohabitation or marriage with this person at this time is right for you.

Then, you can feel confident that, whatever is to come, that the future is in your hands!

The Prenup: An Ounce of Prevention

As difficult as it is to admit, acknowledge it we must: most marriages end in divorce, and each divorce makes it more likely that your next marriage will end in divorce, as well.

Conflicts over money, we've seen, are one of the top reasons for divorce. Since, as I once heard a therapist say, "You can't resolve during divorce the issues you couldn't resolve during the marriage," the couple that has taken time to devise a prenuptial agreement before taking their vows will be exceedingly glad to have that agreement.

I can already see you wringing your hands. "But prenups aren't romantic." Toughen up, buttercup. Marriage is a business arrangement and has been since the beginning of time.

You wouldn't enter a long-term business arrangement with anyone unless you had a contract spelling out expectations, right? You wouldn't buy a house or car, accept a job, or even open a banking account without an agreement stipulating the cost, payment schedule, and penalties for breach of contract.

Marriage is, theoretically, a lifetime contract. And, like any other agreement, you need to know what will happen if the marriage fails. Your opinion on what that should be matters every bit as much as your partner's, no matter who earns or owns more.

But if you're trying to negotiate the division of your joint kingdom during emotionally charged divorce proceedings – even amicable divorces are fraught with emotion – chances are good that you'll wind up giving a major chunk of all you've worked to build not to yourself and not to your spouse, but to attorneys.

"But my fiancé and I are very much aligned when it comes to money," you might think. "We won't fight about it during the marriage, and we won't fight about it if we get divorced."

Don't believe that for a hot minute. I know what I'm talking about. That first husband with whom I navigated the financial waters so smoothly? We didn't have a prenup. When we decided to end the marriage, the money fights began. It's said that divorce brings out the worst in a person, and, boy, was it true in our situation. By the time it was all said and done, we'd fattened the bank accounts of a couple of divorce attorneys in our town.

If you're already married and wishing you'd drawn up a prenup, it's not too late. But post-marital nuptial agreements, or "post-nups" tend to be more difficult to enforce, especially in "community property" states where every asset obtained during the marriage must, by law, be divided equally between the spouses if they divorce.

Prenups not only protect each of the partners in the marriage, but also their children. With so many "blended" families in our culture today, some find it important to protect a part of the estate they acquired before this new marriage so their biological children can inherit it later. A prenup may stipulate that, in case of divorce, the family property that's been handed down through generations will remain the possession of the spouse who originally owned it.

Of course, the person who owns that property may want to make sure that their spouse is taken care of in another way should divorce happen. The prenup can cover that, too – and so can divorce insurance!

The 'Big Day' Doesn't Have to Cost Big

Weddings have gotten more and more lavish. In 2019, the average wedding cost hovered around $28,000. That's nearly as much as a full-time, $15-per-hour employee earns in an entire year.

Yes, you want a memorable occasion. You want your friends and family there as witnesses to your union. You want a beautiful setting, a delicious cake, perhaps a yummy meal, music with dancing, and photos to peruse in the years to come.

What you don't want is for your wedding day to be "unforgettable" because of all the debt you incur.

So, before you call the caterer, take a deep breath, and ask yourself these questions:

What do you picture when you think of the "perfect" wedding?
Which aspect is the most crucial for you? Is it having the perfect ambiance with just the right flowers and lighting? Is it having a killer DJ or live band that keeps you and your guests dancing the night away? Once

you've decided what's the single most important, allocate your budget to that first. Then, figure out how the rest will fit into your spending.

Who do you most want to be there? Limiting your guest count is the most effective way to pare down your wedding costs. Each person equals one invitation, one seat, and one meal, not including the guest they may bring. If money is tight, send invitations only to those you really want to come.

When my spouse Andy and I got engaged, it was the second marriage for us both. We each came to the partnership with plenty of money. Our families were really excited and so looking forward to a big celebration.

But as we began to plan, we realize that neither of us wanted a huge party. So, we planned a small celebration in a city park with our children. We even had two close friends perform the marriage ceremony. Neither Andy nor I wanted to spend a lot of money on a celebration; our life together, we thought, was celebration enough.

Have you thought about all your options?

If the oversized, family-and-friends-wedding isn't in your budget, don't fret about losing out on the "wedding of your dreams." Instead, change your dreams! "Destination" weddings in some exotic locale tend to attract only close family members and a few friends – and let you combine honeymoon and wedding into one trip. Or you might consider a "just the family" wedding, having a private ceremony with a party to come later. Or consider eloping. I know someone who eloped and, knowing the groom's mother would be heartbroken, brought her along to the Justice of the Peace's office.

Even should you decide on the full-meal-deal wedding, you can save yourself a lot of expense and hassle by keeping these pointers in mind:

- **Get your quotes in writing.** Nothing is worse than having your already expensive wedding suddenly increase in value because your contractor raised their rates. Getting their costs in writing will bind them to the rates they promised, reduce your stress, and help you stay within budget.

- **Be organized.** Keep a binder in which to organize your notes, contracts, and other documents. Take copious notes, always. Not only will it help you stay on top of things, avoid stress, and stay within your parameters, your planning notebook can also make for a nice keepsake commemorating the process. Planning your wedding should be enjoyable and give you positive energy. Getting and staying organized can help you keep it fun.

- **Research and develop a budget.** Do research, ask questions, get quotes, and ask advice from your previously married friends (who might have recommendations or horror stories

175

of vendors to stay away from). Whether you are paying for the wedding yourself or getting help, decide how much you are willing to spend. If you must go back and readjust, that's fine, but I suggest that you ask yourself the questions above before doing so. And remember, starting your marriage off in a good financial position is one heck of a wedding gift to yourself and your spouse!

Consent is Sexy

Why is it that we can talk about sex, which is about intimacy between two people, and not about money, which is an object?

It's time we put the "sexy" back into money talk. I mean, what's not thrilling about dreaming and scheming a future together with someone you love?

Although my first marriage ended in divorce, money wasn't why. Neither of us had unresolved issues around money, and so we could talk about our finances openly and honestly.

We even went out on "money dates" at the end of each quarter-year, treating ourselves to dinner out to review our progress in meeting our shared goals and to set new ones for the quarter ahead.

Before meeting, I'd draw up a list of what was important to me – not just money but household, children, fitness, career, our relationship, and anything else that mattered. We'd talk about the items on my list and his, and devise a third list that combined the two, a sort of master list that we would prioritize.

Maybe we'd agree to get new kitchen cupboards. Maybe I'd want a new bicycle to help meet my fitness goals. Maybe he wanted to save for a house on one of our area lakes. For each item that made the master list, we'd set goals and boundaries including how much time, money, and other resources to expend on it.

These dates were enjoyable for us both: they took the drudge work out of budgeting and helped us to get to know each other better. Through them, money brought us closer together by unifying us and our purpose. What's sexier than that?

Using Power Wisely

"Money is power." I'm sure you've heard this saying. It's true in many ways – it gives us power over ourselves and our own lives, for instance. But using money as a power tool in any relationship will damage the relationship, and possibly destroy it.

When I meet with couples in my office, I get a lot of information about the power dynamics in their relationship when I ask how they make financial decisions. Sometimes, the more conservative partner rules the budget with an iron fist. When this occurs, the other partner often will rebel against the strictures by running up a secret credit card bill or even blatantly breaking the "agreement" by gambling or making extravagant purchases.

When partners don't agree in their approach to money, problems can arise. Being able to negotiate and compromise – on both people's parts – is key to success.

If communicating effectively about money or any other aspect of your relationship feels too hard, I suggest you seek professional help. Couples therapy isn't only for marriages in danger of breaking up. A good counselor can help you develop skills that will strengthen your bonds when times are good, as well.

Too Much Togetherness? Try Separate Accounts

Keeping separate accounts is another approach that works for many couples. Yes, that's right. Marriage doesn't automatically mean pooling all your income in joint accounts.

If your views on spending and saving are irreconcilable or if one partner earns a lot more than the other, or if you have any other reasons for separating your incomes, it's perfectly okay to keep separate accounts. Doing so can make paying bills a bit more difficult, but there are workarounds for that, too.

I know a couple in which the man came into the marriage with $1 million in assets and drew income from them, and the woman held down a low paying job. He routinely spent more than he earned, racking up huge credit card bills, but since the card was his alone it wasn't an issue.

The couple also kept separate checking accounts as well as a single household account for budgeted expenses such as their mortgage and utility payments and groceries. His monthly income was higher than hers, so he contributed a larger amount to this account than she did. They were each free to spend the remainder however they chose.

This system isn't perfect. It fails to account for shared goals and a way to save for them, for instance. But it prevented the couple from fighting about money. The financial pressure off, they were more easily able to negotiate and collaborate on unbudgeted expenses, such as an impromptu vacation or when her car broke down and she couldn't afford to pay for it. (Spoiler alert: he was happy to use his credit card.)

If you and your spouse feel more comfortable having joint accounts, I suggest budgeting a certain amount per person for monthly "mad money." That way, no one has to either feel or be deprived. And be sure to agree on which purchases coming out of your joint account should be discussed in advance, anything costing more than, say, $150 or $200.

Suddenly Single: Six Ways to Cope

If your marriage is ending in divorce, you'll be a lot less stressed and better taken care of if you've taken my advice and drawn up a pre-nup with your spouse before the marriage.

If your spouse dies, having participated in drawing up their will can give you peace of mind, knowing what's in it and that you're taken care of.

If you don't have these things, finding yourself suddenly single could be much more painful. And in fact, divorce is nearly as emotionally difficult as losing your loved one to death. Love of others for you and of you for yourself can help you to carry on.

"To plant a seed, we must dig into the dark soil." This saying holds more than a kernel of truth. Even the most devastating occurrences can stimulate new growth—personal, spiritual, and financial—with the proper self-care.

But where to start? Based on my own experiences and others, I've developed these six suggestions to help anyone "suddenly single" recover from loss and carry on:

1. **Embrace change.** Your brain is looking for certainty, which is why an uncertain future can make us feel anxious, or even fearful. However, we can trick our brains by consciously opening our hearts and minds to whatever lies ahead and remembering that we alone have the power to live our lives.

2. **Find support.** If you don't already have a network, consider building one to help you navigate your new life. You will need at least two very close friends, an attorney, a financial advisor, your most immediate family members, and a therapist.

3. **Take care of yourself first.** Get plenty of sleep, exercise, eat healthy foods, and share time with those you can trust. And don't forget to "stop and smell the roses."

4. **Create balance.** Thankfully, a day consists of 24 hours, allowing for eight hours' sleep, eight hours' work, and eight hours' play—a perfect balance.

5. **Dare to dream.** Make a "vision board" on which you write your goals for the next one, five, and ten years, along with pictures that motivate you. Being honest with yourself about your future takes courage, but it does help to move beyond the painful past and into a more positive future.

6. **Take action.** During stressful times, keeping our commitments can feel impossible. I recommend an "action plan," writing down all that you must do and how you will do it. Later, you can review, track your progress, and make changes. This vital step will help you make decisions in your own best interest.

Finding ourselves alone in the world can be scary at first, but it can also, ultimately, be exciting. Tending to ourselves, our daily lives, and our finances in times of grief and loss can empower us to turn the page and start a new chapter in life. Being suddenly single can be a time to reboot and focus on yourself.

Suddenly Single? Find the Support You Need

Losing a spouse, whether to divorce or death, can be the loneliest feeling in the world. It can be downright scary, too, especially for those who depended on their partner to take care of the business that marriage entails.

When we are grieving, tending to such details as the division of assets, wills, and financial investments can feel overwhelming. That's why, even if you, your spouse, and your marriage seem to be in great shape, a little planning can go a long way.

Here are some suggestions for coping after a marriage ends that I relied on while going through my divorce:

- Embrace change

- Find support

- Take care of yourself

- Create balance

- Dare to dream

- Take action

For many, finding support may be the most difficult. How do you build a team of people you trust to help you navigate your new life?

Start with the Foundation

An attorney and a financial advisor are two of the first professionals you should seek.

Whether you're facing divorce or dealing with a deceased spouse's estate, having a reliable, trustworthy attorney who will represent your best interests—not their own—is key to success.

If you live in a small town where the number of divorce attorneys is limited, consider interviewing them all before deciding on one. However, the best way to find a great lawyer may be to get a referral from a trusted source, either someone who's gone through divorce themselves or has close confidants who have. Talk to friends, associates, and colleagues who have been in your situation, and ask whether they would recommend their attorney.

A word of caution: Be wary of lawyers who like to fight. They may (or may not) get a better deal for you, but they will almost certainly increase tensions between you and your ex-to-be, which could be harmful not only to you but also to your children.

Equally important is finding a quality financial adviser. Many people call themselves "financial planners" yet have minimal or no education in the field and lack certification.

Some questions to ask are:

- What kind of college degree does the person have?
- How long have they been in the industry?

- Have any regulatory complaints been filed against them?

- What makes them qualified to give you advice?

- Have they personally ever filed for bankruptcy?

- Which industry licenses do they have, and what regulatory entity regulates them?

- Why did they choose to be in the financial sector?

- How many firms have they been within their career? If there have been many changes, they need to have good reasons why.

Be picky and insist on a college graduate with the CFP® (Certified Financial Planner) certification and at least five years' experience in the field.

Find Someone to Lean On

Divorce is a long emotional and sometimes legal process. I know this from experience.

Use this difficult period as an opportunity to grow and change. This new chapter in your life offers you an opportunity to live life differently.

Your friends can be an enormous help but be careful whom you trust with your feelings.

Don't confide in too many people. You will wear them out, and you may alienate some who want to help but are uncomfortable with your situation. Instead, consider leaning on a few who encourage you and who are loyal and discreet. Be open to their feedback.

We're only as good as the people we surround ourselves with, especially when managing our affairs. "Suddenly single," like parachuting from a plane, can be a terrifying experience or an exhilarating one, depending on your level of preparation and your attitude. For that initial leap, why not go tandem with professionals and advisors whom you can trust with your livelihood, if not with your life?

Suddenly Single:

Do You Need that Big House?

One of the most complex aspects of being "suddenly single" is finding yourself alone in the home you once shared with your spouse and perhaps children. You have the memories, more house, yard, and possessions, perhaps more than you need now. All this stuff takes energy and time to maintain.

Ask yourself: How do you want to spend the rest of your life?

Try this fun (and thought-provoking) trick: estimate the number of years you have left on Earth. Turn those years into days, hours, and minutes.

Now, ask yourself: how do I want to spend this precious time? Is your answer, "Cleaning the house, mowing the lawn, and maintaining my stuff?" I didn't think so.

A home, especially if we've lived there for a long time, can be as much a sentimental object as a shelter. Memories fill every room, turning each into a cherished memento.

But let's be honest: it's the people who made those memories, not the wood, plaster, and glass that make up the house. Who says you would not love another home—one more appropriate for your household size, lifestyle, and income—just as much or even more?

Maybe your house serves as a status symbol, reassuring you and others that you've "made it" in life. Perhaps you felt giddy when you first moved in, thinking, "Look at me now!"

Having a big, beautiful house is the essence of the American dream. Popular culture helps reinforce the notion that "we are what we own."

But houses cost money—the bigger the house, the higher the price. There's always something to be done: appliances break down, a storm damages the roof, squirrels nest in the attic, trees need pruning, or the furnace needs replacing.

Large houses cost more to heat and cool, more to insure, and their taxes are higher. Meanwhile, rooms languish, empty and unused. Is this the best use of your money?

Finding yourself unexpectedly alone is incredibly stressful. Why add to your worries with the endless list of chores and expenses a big house incurs? Selling your home and turning the proceeds into liquid investments means you can use your money whenever and however you wish, offering real peace of mind.

Take Action: the 1-2-3 of Downsizing

1. **Purge.** Clearing your closets, drawers, shelves, and basement of items you don't use or need can be liberating. You'll feel lighter, as if bailing out a too-heavy vessel.

   After you've finished, you'll have things that *you own*, consciously and by choice, not an overload of possessions that own *you*.

2. **Test the waters.** Check out some smaller homes for sale or rent, whether houses, condos, or apartments. Make a list of features that you love about your current home or wish you had. A sunny breakfast nook? A shady yard? A modern kitchen? View only places that meet your criteria and see if any excite you.

Talk to a financial planner. Should you buy or rent? How much should you pay? Conventional wisdom says no more than 28 percent of monthly income should go to housing. If you reduce your costs, what might you do with the extra money? Invest, travel, give to your children, and give to charity? All of the above? A financial planner can help you to use your funds wisely and live the life you truly want.

Change is complex, and even more so when it happens suddenly and unexpectedly. You may feel out of control—but this feeling will pass. Once you're ready to take the reins, asking how much house you need and want is a significant first step.

Chapter 8

SELF-ACTUALIZE

"No matter who you are, no matter what you did, no matter where you've come from, you can always change, become a better version of yourself."
~Madonna

Now is when the fun begins.

Yes, maybe a bit of discomfort, too, at first, as you shine a light on hidden aspects of yourself, but mostly pleasure. The pleasure of getting to know yourself better and finding out what makes you tick, the pleasure of dreaming big dreams for your life, the joys of living each day in confidence that your financial house is in order, the thrill of feeling the love for yourself that well-thought-out, planned purchases represent, with a joyous "Yes!" rather than the furtive, impulsive buys that can later bring shame.

And best of all, the confidence that comes from being on the path to financial freedom.

You've Got This!

At the time of this writing, I was listening to Dr. Shefali Tsabary's *book A Radical Awakening,* and thinking of you. In it, the author explores many of the themes that I've discussed here: moving from a patriarchal mindset (which, by the way, is toxic for men, too) into one of self-respect, self-empowerment, and self-love.

To move from fear into love, however, you need one critical ingredient: curiosity.

Curiosity takes us out of our negative feelings and into a more detached state in which we act as the observer of our own lives, attitudes, choices, and emotions. Curiosity has us asking, "Why does this trigger me?" so that we can move out of the triggered state into one of understanding and self-compassion. Curiosity can move us from fear into love.

No matter where you are on your life's path, no matter your age or circumstances, it's never too early or too late to start the journey away from fear – including fear of money – toward love. As you progress, you may find that every aspect of your life gets shinier, sunnier, warmer. Keeping your journal, reflecting on all the reasons you have for gratitude, setting boundaries for yourself with yourself and others, and all the other actions called for throughout this book culminate in a single purpose: a life of abundance and love. *Your* life of abundance and love.

How you interact with your money reflects how you feel about yourself. After all, you earned it, and so it's now an aspect of you –

your reward for the work you did to merit it. Will you treat it as a reward and use it accordingly to enrich your life, or will you throw it away on people who don't deserve it or items that you don't need or even really want?

The choice is yours. One choice represents self-respect and self-love, and the other, a lack of both. "It's a journey, not a destination" has become an overused phrase, to the point where it almost has no meaning. In this case, however, it rings true.

As long as you have money, you will need to manage it. To do so in a self-responsible, self-loving, and self-respecting way, you must truly own your money, respect it, and love it… which means owning, respecting, and loving yourself. When you give ownership, respect, and love to your financial life, they will come back to you.

The Time Is Now

Talking about self-love seems so narcissistic in this day and age. But let's consider the origin of the word "narcissism." It stems from the Greek mythological tale of Narcissus, a handsome youth who caught his reflection for the first time in a pool of water and became entranced. He fell so completely in love that, when he finally realized what it was – an image of himself – he despaired and killed himself.

The reason he was so upset, I think, was that Narcissus had never loved anyone. He was such a beautiful youth that many people fell in love with him, but he scorned and disdained them all. Even a lovely nymph had thrown her arms around him in a fit of passion, but he'd pushed her away so roughly that she'd wandered the woods crying until nothing but her sobs remained. Her name was Echo.

Narcissists, then, love themselves pretty much to the exclusion of everyone else. They don't have problems with people who beg or manipulate them for money (or as I call them, "money vampires") because they are neither generous, empathetic, or sympathetic to others. With narcissists, it's all about them.

Self-love is different. It is the healthy development of a relationship with your real self – not your mirror image, which is all projection and outward, rather than inward, reflection. In this relationship, you come first not because you're self-centered, but because taking care of ourselves is our primary task in life. It's the one thing that no one, no matter how much they might wish to, can do for us.

"You're thinking only of yourself," a friend's husband snarled as they negotiated their divorce.

"Well, if I don't think about me, then who will?" she said. Indeed.

Self-love means taking charge of yourself and your money. After all, you've worked for everything that you have, whether you realize it or not. Even inherited money has its invisible strings. And you will continue to work, hopefully until you've set yourself up to retire.

You are the one responsible for doing this – no one else. Prince Charming isn't going to rescue you. You stand a much greater chance of being struck by lightning than of winning the lottery. This is your one life (as far as we know). This life represents your one opportunity to live. Your destiny is in your hands, alone.

What Are You Waiting For?

Have you ever known people who parted from their spouse but never divorced? Ask them why and they'll give you excuses: the spouse needs the health insurance, they don't want to traumatize the children, the finances are too entangled to divide without devastating one of or both their lives, and so forth.

Alternatively, someone who has only a minority share in a business venture will never have any control over the company or be able to influence its decisions. Why not move on, or challenge the status quo, or start your own business? Taking an active role in your life is always better than resigning yourself to a passive one.

Humans are really, really good at stasis. Change is hard. So, we delay it, sometimes for as long as we can. In the meantime, life is passing us by, as well as opportunities that we can't seize while we are stuck in the quagmire in which we placed ourselves.

Your future should always be brighter than your past. Isn't that what you want for yourself? You are the only one who can make it come true.

Lean into Your Fears

Fear can be paralyzing – or it can be energizing. The choice is yours.

When you have a health problem, what do you do? I know someone who developed sciatica, which is a bunching in the hip muscles that irritates the sciatic nerve. The pain was so excruciating that she couldn't sit down for weeks. She cried, telling her partner that, at forty, she was already an "old lady." She was afraid that her condition might be permanent.

But she didn't let this problem get her down for long. She went to see an exercise physiologist who taught her the stretches that she does to this day to keep sciatica at bay. She also began a physician fitness routine that has the added benefit of improving her overall health.

"When I feel fear or anxiety, I know it's a signal that I need to take action," she said.

The same is true of financial fears. If you feel afraid to look at your bank accounts or credit card bill, take action with a budget that you stick to. If you fear growing older because you don't have enough money to cover medical bills or to retire, cut back on something, go back to school to train for a better-paying job, or learn how to negotiate a raise at the job you have so you can start building your accounts.

The trick is to make an action plan and stick to it. And if you fall, get right back up and pick up where you left off – or, if necessary, start over again.

I know a woman who, at 34, wants to get married and have children. Her boyfriend of six years said he wanted the same thing, but he hadn't proposed. She was becoming fearful that she would soon be too old to start a family. But – why is she waiting for him? She could propose marriage, and if he says no, move on. Or she could simply free herself to find someone who wants to start a family with her now.

So, what is she doing? None of these things. She continues to wait, hoping that he'll come around. Her fear of being alone is so great that it's boxed her in like a barbed-wire fence.

What's really hard about this situation is her vulnerability to him. If he leaves her, she'll be alone, anyway – and if he waits long enough before doing so, it may be too late for her to have the child or children she wants so badly. Only by taking action now will she have the chance to attain her heart's desire.

I've met plenty of women who remain in unhappy marriages not for emotional reasons, but for financial ones. They aren't afraid to be alone, but to be destitute. Their fear is a sign that something is wrong in their lives. They need to find a path to self-sufficiency – even if they decide to stay married forever.

Here's a secret that men have always known that a lot of women never imagined: being able to take care of yourself is the ultimate superpower. Not developing this superpower is like being a bird that never flies – or, worse, that won't leave its cage.

Fear keeps us tethered, small, and miserable. Isn't it time you conquered your fears and started living life?

If you need help moving forward, meeting with a professional can give you the insights and tools you need. A therapist might help you understand the source of your fears, which, as we saw in Chapter One, can enable you to resolve them, lightening your load so that your first step feels possible.

An attorney can help you to understand the practical implications of taking that step, whether it's entering a marriage or leaving one, starting your own business, or something else, so that you can determine how to prepare and protect yourself.

A financial advisor can help you write your money map to achieving what you want to accomplish in life, in the near, short, and long terms. This person can work with you individually or, if you're partnered, you and your significant other.

Ultimately, though, they can't do the work for you. The awesome responsibility for your self-actualization lies with you and you alone. Mastering your fears, including your money fears, is something that only you can do. It's something you *must* do if you are to live your best life.

Actions Speak Louder than Feelings

Did you know that if you want to bring some joy into someone else's life, all you need to do is give them a moment of your attention and a compliment?

When is the last time that you have done this for yourself?

When was the last time you took a moment to give yourself that kind of focus, and to recognize something you have done right or that you are proud of in your life?

Ninety-five percent of our decisions have a purely emotional basis, according to the research of neuroscientist Antonio Damasio. Rather than thinking and then acting, he found, we tend to feel first, and then act.

Damasio's research studied brain-damaged people who were unable to experience emotions. These people could logically think through a situation and list out the pros and cons of a problem, but could not execute and decide after their analysis.

Damasio's conclusions from his research? "Humans are not either thinking machines or feeling machines but rather feeling machines that think."

Being machines of a sort, however, we can tinker with the mechanism behind our feelings. We can, in effect, quieten them to give our rational, goal-oriented prefrontal cortex a chance to be heard as well.

To do so, you need first to sit with your feelings. When you feel yourself in an emotional state such as anxiety, fear, or dread, give yourself a "time out" to sit quietly with your eyes closed, take some deep breaths, and concentrate on what you're feeling and thinking. Use your imagination, release your inhibitions, and really give your feelings and their associated thoughts full rein. After a minute or two, you may find that they begin to lose their intensity, little by little, until your mind has become completely calm.

This technique works in part because of the effects of deep breathing on our brains and our bodies. "Deep breathing increases the supply of oxygen to your brain and stimulates the parasympathetic nervous system, which promotes a state of calmness," writes the American Institute of Stress.

When we make decisions purely from an emotional state, not using our rational mind, we tend to act impulsively, as children do whose prefrontal cortexes have yet to fully develop. Pausing and giving our rational minds a voice not only calms us but helps us to make wiser decisions.

From Fear to Love in 8 Self-Actualizing Steps

Self-actualization is "the complete realization of one's potential, and the full development of one's abilities and appreciation for life." It's at the top of Maslow's Hierarchy of Needs, which we can think of as ladder whose rungs must be climbed one at a time before we can reach the top.

At the bottom of the hierarchy are our basic, foundational needs such as food, water, and shelter. Next is safety; then love and belonging, then esteem. Before we reach self-actualization, Maslow wrote, we must first fulfill all the needs under it.

With so many needs to fulfill first, it's a wonder that anyone reaches self-actualization. In fact, most people never do. But *you* can. Your money journey from fear to love can help take you to the very top.

Self-actualization is what this book is really all about. By following the eight steps outlined in its eight chapters, you'll find yourself growing and changing and developing into that confident, joyous, self-fulfilled person you've always wanted to become. As a reminder, I'll list them here:

1. Get curious. In your journal, write about your past, your present, and your future with an eye to self-discovery. The more you know about yourself, the more you can grow.

2. Empathize with yourself. Rather than judging yourself for your actions, try to understand why you do what you do and decide which behaviors you want to change. Be prepared to stumble; you are human, after all.

3. Get organized. Clean out the clutter in your life and your financial life. Get out of debt, set a budget, and more. Doing so clears your mindset and your life, like clearing and leveling the land on which you'll build the beautiful structure that will be your life from now on.

4. Chart your course. Using the exercises in this book, write out your plan for where you want to go and how you will get there. Make sure you make the journey as much fun as possible! You won't come this way again.

5. Add it up. List your monthly sources of income and expenses as well as your assets and liabilities. As you begin to turn the red columns to black, you'll see all aspects of your life turning around, including your frown.

6. Do your money-dos. Getting to financial freedom – an aspect of self-actualization – requires nurturing and maintenance. Set up automatic payments to your investment accounts, check your budget and spending weekly if not daily, and keep journaling and dreaming.

7. Mind your relationships. We can only love others as much as we love ourselves, and setting boundaries in our relationships with others is an essential form of self-love and self-respect.

8. Live your best life. Need I say more?

Actively investing in yourself is the fastest, most authentic way to self-actualization. Make your best life happen, rather than drifting along and waiting for things to happen to you. It takes time, effort, money, commitment, and a willingness to grow parts of yourself that are undeveloped. Why not start now?

Every day – every hour; every minute – brings a chance to be different. You get to choose.

Every day brings opportunity for change.

Every day brings a new opportunity to be better.

Every day brings a new opportunity to do better.

This is your life. You've got this!

Today is *your* day.

AFTERWORD

I wrote this book to help you on your journey, but writing it was part of mine – a process of becoming and discovering what's been inside me most of my life, and one that I wanted to share with you.

For you, I hope that along these eight steps on your path, you, too, can find your way from shame to joy, and from fear to love. Taking even small steps of curiosity will unleash your wonder.

I hope you will take that first action that will help you observe your choices from a different perspective – and perhaps choose a new path that values *you*. Life is too short for worry about scarcity. Too often, we think we'll have more time and more options later if we deal with another person's needs, whether that be a child, partner, or boss. Too often, we have nothing left after giving away our time, talent, and energy.

I hope you can find yourself by taking actions via your finances that will give you options to enjoy your life now and long into your future. Empowerment truly is about taking control of your time and where you spend it, and who you spend it on.

As you embark on this exciting, rewarding journey, I wish these three outcomes for you:

1. You take an honest look at the good, the bad, and the ugly of your financial life right now.

2. You have compassion for yourself and understand your journey and conditioning that have brought you to your current situation.

3. You have defined goals to work toward and become empowered with your very first steps to your future.

We all make choices, and I intend to make you aware of yours. Spending my career helping clients reach their goals, watching their self-confidence grow, their quality of life unfold into excellent options has indeed been an honor. I feel so grateful to be a part of their journey, and of yours. Sharing these ideas and steps with you is my way of helping to free more people from their limiting beliefs.

Thank you for taking the time to engage with me here. I invite you to make this a two-way conversation. Let me know of your ideas and any changes that might occur on your journey. You can reach me at scarlson@fulcrumfinancialgroup or through our website at www.fulcrumfinancialgroup.com.

I also encourage you to work with a coach, a financial advisor, and a trusted friend. They can help you get organized and build your boundaries and respect for your financial life.

Just know that change is hard, and that any step of transition towards your fantastic future is in the right direction, regardless of how small it is.

I am in awe of you and know your future is brighter than your past. Thank you for taking your first important step, and for bringing me along.

Kindly,
Sarah

The opinions voiced in this material are for general information only and are not intended to provide specific advice or recommendations for any individual. To determine which strategies or investments may be suitable for you, consult the appropriate qualified professional prior to making a decision.

All investing involves risk including loss of principal. No strategy assures success or protects against loss. There is no guarantee that a diversified portfolio will enhance overall returns or outperform a non-diversified portfolio. Diversification does not protect against market risk.

Stock investing includes risks, including fluctuating prices and loss of principal.

Investing in mutual funds involves risk, including possible loss of principal. Fund value will fluctuate with market conditions and it may not achieve its investment objective.

Dollar cost averaging involves continuous investment in securities regardless of fluctuation in price levels of such securities. An investor should consider their ability to continue purchasing through fluctuating price levels. Such a plan does not assure a profit and does not protect against loss in declining markets.

CDs are FDIC insured to specific limits and offer a fixed rate of return if held to maturity, whereas investing in securities is subject to market risk including loss of principal.

Dividend payments are not guaranteed and may not be reduced or eliminated at any time by the company.

Traditional IRA account owners have considerations to make before performing a Roth IRA conversion. These primarily include income tax consequences on the converted amount in the year of conversion, withdrawal limitations from a Roth IRA, and income limitations for 20future contributions to a Roth IRA. In addition, if you are required to take a required minimum distribution (RMD) in the year you convert, you must do so before converting to a Roth IRA.

A Roth IRA offers tax deferral on any earnings in the account. Qualified withdrawals of earnings from the account are tax-free. Withdrawals of earning prior to the age 59 ½ or prior to the account being opened for 5 years, whichever is later, may result in a 10 % IRS penalty tax. Limitations and restrictions may apply.

CPSIA information can be obtained
at www.ICGtesting.com
Printed in the USA
LVHW100811011022
729705LV00004B/16